FINES AND RESTITUTIONS IN FEDERAL CRIMINAL CASES

FINES AND RESTITUTIONS IN FEDERAL CRIMINAL CASES

PETER N. ALLERTON JR.
EDITOR

Nova Science Publishers, Inc.
New York

For permission to use material from this book please contact us:
Telephone 631-231-7269; Fax 631-231-8175
Web Site: http://www.novapublishers.com

LIBRARY OF CONGRESS CATALOGING-IN-PUBLICATION DATA

ISBN: 978-1-60456-589-8

Published by Nova Science Publishers, Inc. New York

Contents

PREFACE

Restitution is the act of restoring an individual or entity in whole or in part to the lost circumstances they might have once enjoyed. In a federal criminal context, it is the order of a sentencing court directing a defendant to reimburse or otherwise compensate the victims of his crimes. Restitution is based on the losses suffered by the victims of a crime. Neither the defendant's financial condition at the time of sentencing, nor his future economic prospects figure in the amount of restitution awarded.

Consequently, in some cases the amount of restitution ordered may exceed what the defendant can ever reasonably be expected to pay, particularly in the case of mandatory restitution. Nevertheless, there have been suggestions that in other instances insufficient restitution has been ordered or collected because of the particularities of restitution law.

Chapter 1 - Federal courts may not order a defendant to pay restitution to the victims of his or her crimes unless authorized to do so. Several statutes supply such authorization. For instance, federal courts are statutorily required to order victim restitution when sentencing a defendant for a felony that constitutes either a crime of violence or an offense against property, including fraud or deceit proscribed in Title 18 of the *United States Code*. The obligation exists even if the defendant is indigent, and restitution must take the form of in-kind or installment payments. Moreover, a court may not order restitution as required by the statute and then grant the defendant remission of restitution. Ordinarily, however, restitution is available only to victims who have suffered a physical injury or financial loss as a direct and proximate consequence of the crime of conviction, and only to the extent of their losses. In addition, federal courts are permitted to order victim restitution when sentencing a defendant for various controlled substance and aviation safety offenses, or any felony proscribed in Title 18 for which restitution is not mandatory. Moreover, a federal court may make restitution a condition of probation or supervised release.

When restitution is to be ordered, a probation officer prepares a report after gathering information from victims, the government, and the defendant. The parties receive copies of the report and may contest its recommendations. The court has considerable discretion as to the manner and scheduling of restitution payments, but the authority may not be delegated to probation or prison officials. Furthermore, the order must provide for full restitution for all victims unless the sheer number of victims or the complications of a given case preclude such an order.

Under the abatement doctrine, when a defendant dies before his or her appeal has become final, the law treats the indictment and conviction as though it had never happened. The conviction is vacated and the indictment dismissed. The courts do not agree on whether the doctrine also reaches unfulfilled obligations under a restitution order.

This report is available in an abridged form — without footnotes, citations to most authorities, or appendices — as CRS Report RS22708, *Restitution in Federal Criminal Cases: A Sketch.* Related reports include CRS Report RL34139, *Criminal Restitution Proposals in the 110th Congress*, available in abridged form as CRS Report RS22709, *Criminal Restitution in the 110th Congress: A Sketch.*

Chapter 2 - Restitution legislation in the 110th Congress falls into three categories. Some proposals, such as the gang crime bills, create new federal crimes or amend specific existing federal offenses and in doing so include specific restitution provisions particular to those offenses, e.g., H.R. 880, H.R. 1582, H.R. 1692, S. 456, and S. 990 (gang bills); and H.R. 871 (spousal support). Other proposals address a particular aspect of the law such as abatement which limits restitution collection after the defendant's death (S. 149). Two bills — H.R. 845, the Criminal Restitution Improvement Act, and S. 973, the Restitution for Victims of Crime Act — make substantial changes in federal restitution law. The proposals call for three kinds of adjustments: (1) an expansion of offenses for which restitution may be ordered without recourse to the laws relating to probation and supervised release; (2) an overhaul of the procedures governing the issuance and enforcement of restitution orders to afford prosecutors greater enforcement flexibility without having to seek the approval of the sentencing court; and (3) authority for preindictment and presentencing restraining orders and other protective measures to prevent dissipation of assets by those who may subsequently owe restitution. Although similar in many respects, S. 973 more closely resembles the proposals transmitted by the Justice Department. The provisions of H.R. 845 also appear as Title V of the Violent Crime Control Act of 2007 (H.R. 3156/S. 1860).

This is an abridged version of CRS Report RL34139, *Criminal Restitution Proposals in the 110th Congress*. Related reports include CRS Report RL34138, *Restitution in Federal Criminal Cases*, and CRS Report RS22708, *Restitution in Federal Criminal Cases: A Sketch*, by Charles Doyle.

Chapter 3 - Federal courts may not order a defendant to pay restitution to the victims of his or her crimes unless authorized to do so. Several statutes supply such authorization. For instance, federal courts are statutorily required to order victim restitution when sentencing a defendant for a felony that constitutes either a crime of violence or an offense against property, including fraud or deceit proscribed in title 18 of the United States Code. The obligation exists even if the defendant is indigent, and restitution must take the form of in-kind or installment payments. Moreover, a court may not order restitution as required by the statute and then grant the defendant remission of restitution. Ordinarily, however, restitution is available only to victims who have suffered a physical injury or financial loss as a direct and proximate consequence of the crime of conviction, and only to the extent of their losses. In addition, federal courts are permitted to order victim restitution when sentencing a defendant for various controlled substance and aviation safety offenses, or any felony proscribed in Title 18 of the *United States Code* for which restitution is not mandatory. Moreover, a federal court may make restitution a condition of probation or supervised release.

When restitution is to be ordered, a probation officer prepares a report after gathering information from victims, the government, and the defendant. The parties receive copies of the report and may contest its recommendations. The court has considerable discretion as to the manner and scheduling of restitution payments, but the authority may not be delegated to probation or prison officials. Furthermore, the order must provide for full restitution for all victims unless the sheer number of victims or the complications of a given case preclude such an order.

This is an abridged version of a longer report, CRS Report RL34138, *Restitution in Federal Criminal Cases*, without the footnotes and citations to authority found in the longer report. Related reports include CRS Report RL34139, *Criminal Restitution Proposals in the 110th Congress*, available in an abridged version as CRS Report RS22709, *Criminal Restitution in the 110th Congress: A Sketch*, all by Charles Doyle.

In: Fines and Restitutions...
Editor: P. N. Allerton Jr., pp. 1-50
ISBN: 978-1-60456-589-8

Chapter 1

RESTITUTION IN FEDERAL CRIMINAL CASES*

Charles Doyle
American Law Division

ABSTRACT

Federal courts may not order a defendant to pay restitution to the victims of his or her crimes unless authorized to do so. Several statutes supply such authorization. For instance, federal courts are statutorily required to order victim restitution when sentencing a defendant for a felony that constitutes either a crime of violence or an offense against property, including fraud or deceit proscribed in Title 18 of the *United States Code*. The obligation exists even if the defendant is indigent, and restitution must take the form of in-kind or installment payments. Moreover, a court may not order restitution as required by the statute and then grant the defendant remission of restitution. Ordinarily, however, restitution is available only to victims who have suffered a physical injury or financial loss as a direct and proximate consequence of the crime of conviction, and only to the extent of their losses. In addition, federal courts are permitted to order victim restitution when sentencing a defendant for various controlled substance and aviation safety offenses, or any

---

* Excerpted from CRS Report RL34138, dated August 17, 2007.

felony proscribed in Title 18 for which restitution is not mandatory. Moreover, a federal court may make restitution a condition of probation or supervised release.

When restitution is to be ordered, a probation officer prepares a report after gathering information from victims, the government, and the defendant. The parties receive copies of the report and may contest its recommendations. The court has considerable discretion as to the manner and scheduling of restitution payments, but the authority may not be delegated to probation or prison officials. Furthermore, the order must provide for full restitution for all victims unless the sheer number of victims or the complications of a given case preclude such an order.

Under the abatement doctrine, when a defendant dies before his or her appeal has become final, the law treats the indictment and conviction as though it had never happened. The conviction is vacated and the indictment dismissed. The courts do not agree on whether the doctrine also reaches unfulfilled obligations under a restitution order.

This report is available in an abridged form — without footnotes, citations to most authorities, or appendices — as CRS Report RS22708, *Restitution in Federal Criminal Cases: A Sketch*. Related reports include CRS Report RL34139, *Criminal Restitution Proposals in the 110th Congress*, available in abridged form as CRS Report RS22709, *Criminal Restitution in the 110th Congress: A Sketch*.

INTRODUCTION

Federal courts may not order a defendant to pay restitution to the victims of his or her crimes unless authorized to do so.[1] Several statutes supply such authorization. Thus, federal courts are statutorily required to order victim restitution when sentencing a defendant for a felony that constitutes either

- a crime of violence;[2]
- an offense against property, including fraud or deceit proscribed in Title 18;[3]
- maintaining a drug-involved premises;[4]
- animal enterprise terrorism;[5]
- failure to provide child support;[6]
- human trafficking;[7]

- sexual abuse;[8]
- sexual exploitation of children;[9]
- stalking or domestic violence;[10]
- telemarketing fraud;[11] or
- amphetamine or methamphetamine offenses.[12]

The obligation exists even if the defendant is indigent, and restitution must take the form of in-kind or installment payments.[13] Moreover, a court may not order restitution as required by the statute and then grant the defendant remission of restitution.[14] Ordinarily, however, restitution is available only to victims who have suffered a physical injury or financial loss as a direct and proximate consequence of the crime of conviction, and only to the extent of their losses.[15]

In addition, federal courts are permitted to order victim restitution when sentencing a defendant for various controlled substance and aviation safety offenses, or any felony proscribed in Title 18 of the *United States Code* for which restitution is not mandatory.[16] Moreover, a federal court may make restitution a condition of probation or supervised release.[17]

BACKGROUND

The origins of restitution are diverse. Grounded in fairness[18] and often thought of as an equitable remedy,[19] its antecedents can be easily found in law as well.[20] As its name implies, restitution restores the victim to the status quo ante, that is, making the depleted victim whole again.[21] Restitution has been a feature of the federal system of criminal justice for close to a century. In its earliest form, it was an unwritten feature of an underwritten system of probation and suspended sentences.[22] Then in 1916, the Supreme Court held that the lower federal courts had no inherent power to suspend sentences.[23] Congress responded by granting the courts explicit authority to suspend sentences and to place defendants on probation.[24] In doing so, the courts were permitted to require probationers "to pay in one or several sums a fine imposed at the time of being placed on probation and ... to make restitution or reparation to the aggrieved party or parties for actual damages or loss caused by the offense for which conviction was had, and ... to provide for the support of any person or persons for whose support" they were "legally responsible."[25] This authority continued essentially unchanged for more than 50 years.[26] Even though the federal courts enjoy no other power to order restitution in a criminal case,[27] the authority was "infrequently used and indifferently enforced."[28]

Congress found this situation unsatisfactory.[29] Thus, in the Victim and Witness Protection Act of 1982 (VWPA), it vested federal courts with the general discretion to order restitution in any criminal case arising out of Title 18 of the *United States Code* or in air piracy cases.[30] In the Violent Crime Control and Law Enforcement Act of 1994, Congress established mandatory restitution as a feature of the federal criminal prohibitions on sexual abuse, sexual exploitation of children, and domestic violence.[31] Then, in the Mandatory Victim Restitution Act (MVRA) portion of the Antiterrorism and Effective Death Penalty Act of 1996, Congress made mandatory restitution a consequence of conviction in most serious federal criminal cases (i.e., crimes of violence and, when proscribed in Title 18 of the *United States Code*, crimes against property, including fraud).[32]

CONSTITUTIONAL CONSIDERATIONS

Restitution's uncertain ancestry — equitable and legal, civil and criminal — has given rise to a number of constitutional challenges over the years. Some initially saw restitution as an alternative to civil litigation on behalf of the victims of crime. If this were the case, defendants claimed that they should enjoy a Seventh Amendment right to have a jury determine the facts upon which a restitution order was based. Their challenges came to naught. The Supreme Court has said that the Seventh Amendment extends only to civil actions similar to those tried before a jury when the Amendment was ratified in 1791.[33] The lower courts rejected the Seventh Amendment challenges either because they concluded that restitution was a criminal rather than a civil sanction or because, at common law, restitution was not a matter presented to a jury; in some cases, the challenges were rejected for both reasons.[34]

However, if restitution is a criminal sanction, must it observe the constitutional restrictions on sanctions, such as the proscriptions on ex post facto laws, excessive fines, and cruel and unusual punishments? If the Seventh Amendment right to a jury trial in civil cases has no bearing, what of the Sixth Amendment right to a jury trial in criminal cases?

On the question of retroactive application of new laws and the ex post facto clause, there is no consensus among the lower federal appellate courts, although a majority take the position that the clause applies and, consequently, exposure to increased restitution liability may not be applied retroactively.[35]

The scant case law available on the issue indicates that the Eighth Amendment's excessive fines clause, as well as its cruel and unusual punishment clause, marks the outer bounds of the courts' restitution authority.[36] These limitations, however, impose no real impediments. They condemn fines and punishments that are grossly disproportionate,[37] although, by definition, restitution must be exactly proportionate to the harm caused by the offense.[38]

In those federal circuits where restitution is considered a criminal penalty, questions regarding the Sixth Amendment right to jury trial are raised. In a series of cases beginning with *Apprendi v. New Jersey[39]* and culminating in *United States v. Booker*,[40] the Supreme Court held that the Sixth Amendment right to a jury trial and the Fifth Amendment right to due process require that "any fact (other than a prior conviction) which is necessary to support a sentence exceeding the maximum authorized by the facts established by a plea of guilty or a jury verdict must be admitted by the defendant or proved to a jury beyond a reasonable doubt."[41]

Restitution, on the other hand, is determined by the court on the basis of a preponderance of the evidence. Nevertheless, the lower federal appellate courts have rejected arguments that the *Apprendi* line of cases clouds the validity of a restitution order under such circumstances — either because restitution does not constitute a criminal sanction and thus raises no Sixth Amendment concerns or because the restitution statutes fail to set the "statutory maximum" necessary to trigger *Apprendi* concerns.[42]

None of the due process and equal protection challenges have thus far survived appellate scrutiny.[43]

VICTIMS

The various federal restitution statutes address three questions: Who qualifies as a victim? What crimes trigger restitution authority? What type of injuries or losses does restitution cover? As originally cast, Section 3663 (VWPA) authorized restitution for "any victim" of any crime proscribed in Title 18 of the *United States Code*, but did not define "victim."[44] The Supreme Court read the statute narrowly and held that it authorized restitution only for the crime of conviction; it did not authorize restitution for related charges dropped as part of a plea agreement.[45] Congress responded almost immediately with a more explicit statement of section 3663's coverage.[46] It replicated and enlarged that statement when it enacted Section 3663A six years later.[47]

Sections 3663 and 3663A authorize restitution orders for the benefit of the victims of the crime of conviction;[48] however, the term *victim* is expressly defined (i.e., "a person directly and proximately harmed as a result of the commission of an offense"). The term *victim* also includes someone harmed by a scheme, conspiracy, or pattern of activity that is an element of the crime of conviction.[49] Sections 3663 and 3663A twice describe the circumstances under which representatives and others may stand in the shoes of a victim.[50] Finally, the sections permit restitution orders for the benefit of anyone identified in a plea agreement.[51]

Although a victim must be a "person" and governmental entities are ordinarily not considered persons,[52] state, local, and federal governmental entities are entitled to restitution orders when they otherwise qualify as victims of a crime under Sections 3663 and 3663A.[53]

On the other hand, although the courts enjoy authority to order restitution paid to family members on behalf of the victims of crime,[54] it is unclear whether the victimization of one member of a family constitutes victimization of its other members sufficient to warrant a restitution order.[55]

Absent a plea bargain or a scheme, conspiracy, or pattern, there must be a close, unbroken connection between the defendant's crime of conviction and the victim's harm. A person is a victim for purposes of Sections 3663 and 3663A if he or she has been "directly and proximately harmed" as a consequence of the crime of conviction.[56] A person has not been directly and proximately harmed if his or her injury is only remotely attributable to the crime of conviction or attributable, at least in part, to an intervening cause unrelated to that offense.[57] Nevertheless, the courts have approved restitution orders for the harm caused by fleeing bank robbers, rather than the harm caused by the robbery itself.[58]

The definition of a *victim* for purposes of restitution under Sections 3663 and 3663A expands when the crime of conviction has as an element a conspiracy or a scheme or pattern of misconduct.[59] In the case of conspiracy, a defendant may be compelled to make restitution both for the harm caused by his or her own misconduct and for the harm of the foreseeable crimes caused by his or her coconspirators.[60]

As for the scheme and pattern exception, most federal crimes do not list schemes or patterns among their elements, although the mail fraud, wire fraud, and racketeering statutes do.[61] In such cases, restitution may include the losses incurred from a different episode of the scheme than the one mentioned in the indictment.[62] Yet the scheme must be the same; victims entitled to restitution do not include those harmed by an otherwise identical scheme but different in time or place than the crime of conviction.[63]

The courts are divided over which statutes qualify as "scheme, conspiracy or pattern" laws. Some say the scheme or pattern must be an element of the crime of conviction; it is not enough that the defendant's crime involves contrivance or repeated related criminality.[64] Others say it is enough; the statute proscribing the crime of conviction need not use the words, "scheme," or "conspiracy," or "pattern."[65]

Although Sections 3663 and 3663A employ the same definition of *victim*, they do not authorize restitution for the same crimes. The list of crimes for which Section 3663 permits restitution supplements the list for which Section 3663A demands restitution.

CRIMES

Section 3663A (Mandatory Restitution)

The mandatory restitution of Section 3663A applies upon conviction for

- a crime of violence, as defined in Section 16;
- an offense against property under Title 18, or under Section 416(a) of the Controlled Substances Act (21 U.S.C. 856(a)), including any offense committed by fraud or deceit; or
- an offense described in Section 1365 (relating to tampering with consumer products), 18 U.S.C. 3663A(c)(1)(A).

Section 16 describes a crime of violence as either "(a) an offense that has as an element the use, attempted use, or threatened use of physical force against the person or property of another, or (b) any other offense that is a felony and that, by its nature, involves a substantial risk that physical force against the person or property of another may be used in the course of committing the offense." As a matter of application, the courts have found that threats, harboring an illegal alien,[66] burglary, and arson[67] are crimes of violence for purposes of Section 3663A and that false statements are not.[68] Elsewhere, the Supreme Court has explained that "crime of violence as defined by Section 16" does not include crimes committed negligently or accidently, such as driving under the influence.[69] Other courts have said that the term *crime of violence* does not encompass possession of a pipe bomb,[70] reckless vehicular assault,[71] or simple misdemeanor assault,[72] but does include such crimes as unauthorized used of a vehicle.[73]

The controlled substance offense that carries with it a restitution requirement under Section 3663A (21 U.S.C. 856) outlaws maintaining a place where controlled substances are manufactured, stored, or used.[74]

The property damage/fraud predicate in Section 3663A must involve a violation proscribed under Title 18 of the *United States Code* rather than an offense found in another title.[75] Yet, the general conspiracy provision in Title 18 can provide the necessary basis for a mandatory restitution order when the defendant is convicted of conspiracy to commit property damage in violation of a federal law found outside of Title 18.[76]

Limitations

Three restrictions apply to the mandatory restitution authorized for defendants convicted of the predicate offenses listed in Section 3663A(c)(1)(A). First, there must be an identifiable victim who has suffered a physical injury or a pecuniary loss.[77] Second, in the case of the property damage/fraud predicates,[78] restitution need not be ordered when the number of victims makes an order impractical.[79] Third, again in the case of property damage/fraud predicates, restitution need not be ordered when the complexity that restitution would introduce into the sentencing process would represent an undue burden.[80]

Other Restitution Statutes

A few other federal statutes authorize restitution. Most apply the procedures that govern Sections 3663 and 3663A to a narrower range of crimes but a wider range of losses than Sections 3663 and 3663A and their attendant enforcement procedures might otherwise permit. Numbered among these provisions are

- 18 U.S.C. 43 (animal enterprise);
- 18 U.S.C. 228(d) (restitution child support cases);
- 18 U.S.C. 1593 (restitution in cases under chapter 77 relating to peonage, slavery, and trafficking in persons);

- 18 U.S.C. 2248 (restitution in cases under chapter 109A relating to sexual abuse);
- 18 U.S.C. 2259 (restitution in cases under chapter 110 relating to sexual exploitation of children);
- 18 U.S.C. 2264 (restitution in cases under chapter 110A relating to domestic violence and stalking);
- 18 U.S.C. 2327 (restitution in telemarketing fraud cases); and
- 21 U.S.C. 853(q) (restitution in controlled substances cases involving amphetamine and methamphetamine offenses).

Section 3663 (Discretionary Restitution)

Section 3663 authorizes restitution when the defendant has been convicted of a crime proscribed under Title 18 of the *United States Code*.[81] It also authorizes restitution when the defendant is convicted of any of several trafficking offenses under the Controlled Substances Act, or of any of a few air safety prohibitions.[82]

Finally, restitution may be ordered on the basis of any crime as a condition of either probation[83] or supervised release,[84] even with respect to crimes for which restitution is not authorized under any of these sections or under Sections 3663 or 3663A.[85]

LOSSES

The losses for which restitution may be ordered depend on the statute under which restitution is ordered. Sections 3663 and 3663A make separate provisions for property losses and personal injuries.

Property Loss or Damage

Sections 3663 and 3663A

Restitution provisions for property damage and losses are the same under Sections 3663 and 3663A: both call for the return of the property, if that provides full victim restitution, and otherwise for compensatory payments.[86] As a general rule, victims are entitled only to be made whole;

they are not entitled to an award that exceeds their losses unless the statute provides otherwise.[87]

Section 3663 alone provides for restitution for state agencies in certain trafficking cases if there is no other identifiable victim.[88]

Neither section explicitly authorizes restitution for a victim's costs associated with the investigation and prosecution of the offense in property loss cases.[89]

Individual Restitution Sections

Although three of the other statutory restitution provisions contemplate awards to victims for both personal injuries and property loss or damage, the others are more narrowly drafted, at least primarily, to address property loss or damage. The animal enterprise interference section, 18 U.S.C. 43(c), permits a sentencing court to order a defendant convicted of violating its proscriptions to pay restitution for specific kinds of damage (i.e., the cost of repeating disrupted experiments, the loss of farm income, and the costs of economic disruption).[90]

The child support restitution section, 18 U.S.C. 228(d), adopts the procedures of Section 3663A upon conviction for interstate evasion of child support orders.[91] The amount of restitution that must be awarded is determined by reference to a state court support order or by other governing state law[92] and, as such, may include the interest on overdue support payments[93] and support owed after children have reached their majority.[94]

The peonage restitution section, 18 U.S.C. 1593, uses the common definition of *victim[95]* and affords victims of human trafficking offenses[96] a wide range of compensation that, unlike Sections 3663 and 3663A, includes a catch-all clause ensuring compensation for predicate crime-related injuries and losses.[97]

Originally enacted two years before the passage of the mandatory restitution provisions of Section 3663A, the telemarketing fraud restitution statute, 18 U.S.C. 2327, once boasted highly individualistic features.[98] It has since been amended so that its provisions more closely track those of the general restitution provisions for losses caused by predicate crimes.[99]

At first glance, the community restitution found in Section 3663(c) might appear to be a duplicate fine provision. It is based on the extent of the harm caused by various controlled substance offenses[100] but payable under a formula that directs only part of the award to crime victim assistance generally,[101] and only in amounts capped by the fine that the court may impose for commission of the offense.[102] Moreover, at least one court has held that the section authorizes restitution only in those cases where the court actually imposes a fine as well; if the court fails to impose a fine, it may not order community restitution.[103]

The methamphetamine statute, 21 U.S.C. 853(q), is limited to restitution awards in methamphetamine and amphetamine cases, particularly to cover the cleanup cost of closing down illicit amphetamine and methamphetamine production sites.[104] Until recently, the section covered only those convicted of manufacturing offenses and consequently reached attempted manufacture but not possession with intent to distribute.[105] The USA PATRIOT Improvement and Reauthorization Act amended the section so that it now authorizes restitution upon conviction for offenses involving the possession, possession with intent to distribute, or manufacture of amphetamine and methamphetamine.[106]

Personal Injuries

Sections 3663 and 3663A

Sections 3663 and 3663A have parallel provisions governing the restitution for personal injuries that permit, or in the case of Section 3663A require, compensation for medical expenses,[107] rehabilitation,[108] lost income,[109] prosecution participation costs,[110] and funeral expenses in the event the victim is killed.[111]

The medical expenses covered by a restitution order may include those paid on the victim's behalf by a third party,[112] and may include the costs of psychiatric and psychological treatment when the victim has suffered a physical injury.[113] Restitution for lost income extends to both past and future lost income.[114]

Both sections explicitly authorize restitution for a victim's costs associated with the investigation and prosecution of the offense.[115] Awards for investigative and prosecutorial participation may include relocation expenses for threatened victims,[116] compensation for wages lost while the victim assisted in the investigation,[117] and attorneys' fees related to the child recovery efforts of the victim of an international parental kidnaping.[118] The sections mention child care, attendance at judicial proceedings, and other matters that bespeak a human victim, but the courts have made it clear that other victims are likewise entitled to restitution under the provisions.[119] Governmental entities may be entitled to restitution awards when they are the victims of a qualifying offense, but not for the costs of investigating and prosecuting the offense.[120]

Other Restitution Statutes

Prior to passage of the general mandatory restitution authority in Section 3663A, Congress enacted three statutory authorizations for three related small sets of offenses that were otherwise identical. Those authorizations, found in 18 U.S.C. 2248, 2259 and 2264, require the courts to order restitution following conviction for an offense proscribed in chapters 109A (sexual abuse), 110 (sexual exploitation of children), and 110A (domestic violence and stalking), respectively.[121] Other than their designation of predicate offenses, the sections are identical. They each

- insist on restitution of the "full amount of the victim's losses,"[122]
- define "victims" in much the manner of Sections 3663 and 3663A,[123]
- supply a list of losses for which restitution must be ordered,[124]
- make it clear that neither the defendant's poverty nor victim compensation from other sources absolves the court of its obligation to order restitution,[125] and
- otherwise adopt the procedural mechanisms used for restitution under Section 3663A.[126]

The inventory losses for which restitution must be awarded is somewhat unique. Unlike Sections 3663 and 3663A, the three sections on their face do not require bodily injury of the victim as a precondition for the award of lost income or the cost of psychiatric treatments. They also have a catch-all clause that has no counterpart in either Section 3663 or 3663A.[127] On the other hand, unlike Sections 3663 and 3663A, they do not authorize payments to third parties to reimburse them for crime-related treatment of a victim.[128]

PROCEDURE

Except to the limited extent otherwise provided in the individual authorization statutes, Section 3664 supplies the procedure that governs the issuance of restitution orders authorized in Title 18 of the *United States Code*,[129] that is to say, for all but those authorized under 21 U.S.C. 853(q), which it also governs.[130]

The procedure begins upon the conviction of a defendant for a predicate offense, at which point the court directs the probation service to investigate and prepare a report identifying each victim of the offense and the extent of their injuries, damages, or losses.[131] Prosecutors are to provide the probation officer with pertinent information.[132] The officer is also to ask victims to detail the extent and specifics of their predicate crime-related losses.[133] The defendant is obliged to give the officer a complete description of his or her financial situation.[134]

The probation officer's report is presented to the court, the defendant, and the prosecutor. The court resolves contested restitution issues by a preponderance of the evidence[135] following a hearing, at which the prosecution bears the burden of establishing the existence and extent of the victims' losses[136] and the defendant bears the burden of questions regarding his or her finances.[137]

Section 3664 is precise when it describes how the court must frame the restitution order. The order must envision full compensation for the losses of each victim without regard to the financial circumstances of the defendant.[138] In its calculation of the amount, manner, and schedule of payment for each victim, however, the court is to consider the defendant's assets, anticipated future income, and other financial obligations.[139] Compensation may be made in lump sum, in-kind payments; installments; or any combination of such methods of payment.[140] In-kind payments may take the form of a return of lost property, replacement in-kind or otherwise, or personal services.[141] When the defendant's financial condition precludes any alternative, the order may call for nominal periodic payments.[142] Several courts have emphasized the importance of the court's close attention to the restitution payment schedule by prohibiting sentencing courts from initially ordering that restitution be paid immediately when it is readily apparent that the defendant is unable to do so, thereby effectively leaving the task of establishing a payment schedule to the probation officer or the Bureau of Prisons.[143]

The court may not take into account the fact that a victim may have been compensated by insurance, forfeiture, civil litigation, or any other alternative form of compensation of his or her injury, loss, or damage.[144]

When the government and the probation officer have been unable to determine the full extent of victim losses within 10 days prior to sentencing, they are obligated to inform the court.[145] The court is then to set a date for the final determination of victim losses within 90 days of sentencing.[146] Victims have a limited option to present claims for restitution relating to undiscovered losses thereafter.[147]

There has been more than a slight difference of opinion among the lower federal appellate courts as to how these provisions should be applied, particularly in cases where the time lines have not been observed. Some courts view the time limits as jurisdictional and deny lower courts the authority to order restitution beyond the statutory limits.[148] Some consider them akin to statutes of limitation and permit the time periods to be tolled.[149] Others see the time limits as a device designed for the benefit of victims, not defendants, and for them the failure to honor the time limits warrants no relief as long as the victim (or the government in the interest of the victim) has no objection and the defendant is given the opportunity to contest.[150]

The courts are likewise divided over the question of whether the court may order restitution to be paid to the Crime Victims Fund on its own initiative if the victim refuses to accept it.[151]

Should the court determine that more than one defendant contributed to the victim's loss, it may apportion restitution accordingly or it may make the defendants jointly and severally liable.[152] When defendants are made jointly and severally liable, each is liable for the entire amount, but the victim is entitled to no more than what is required to be made whole, regardless of what portion each of the defendants ultimately contributes.[153]

Section 3664(i) declares that when it comes to restitution, the United States is to be served last.[154] The provision is cited most often to confirm that under the appropriate circumstances, the government and its departments and agencies may be considered victims for restitution purposes.[155] Where the government is not a victim, however, the forfeiture laws may operate to deplete any assets from which restitution might otherwise have been paid. On the other hand, the defendant is not entitled to have the restitution award offset by the value of any forfeited property, unless the victim is the governmental entity for whose benefit the property is confiscated.[156]

Section 3664(j) permits a court to order restitution to third parties who, as insurers or otherwise, have assumed some or all of the victim's losses, although in such cases, the victim must be fully compensated first.[157] Section 3664(j) also supplies the only explicit offset for the defendant's restitution obligations. A restitution award may be reduced after issuance by any amounts that the victim later receives in the course of related federal or state civil litigation.[158]

The victim, the defendant, or the government may seek to have a restitution order amended to reflect the defendant's changed economic circumstances.[159] The changed economic circumstances envisioned in Section 3664(k) do not include anticipated future changes[160] nor a later, better-informed understanding of the defendant's financial condition at the time of sentence.[161]

There are several means to enforce a restitution order. When restitution is a condition of probation or supervised release, failure to make restitution may provide the grounds for revocation.[162] Moreover, a restitution order operates as a lien on the defendant's property that remains in effect for 20 years.[163] The government may also use garnishment and the other collection mechanisms of the Federal Debt Collection Procedures Act to enforce a restitution order.[164] A victim may use a restitution order to secure a lien against the defendant's property to ensure the payment of restitution.[165] In addition, the victims' rights provisions of 18 U.S.C. 3771 entitle a victim to "full and timely restitution as provided in law," a right the section makes enforceable through a liberalized form of mandamus.[166]

In most instances, a victim may also sue the defendant based on the conduct that led to the conviction and the issuance of the restitution order. During the course of such civil litigation, the defendant may be precluded from denying the facts that formed the basis of the conviction.[167]

Abatement

In a criminal law context, the lower federal courts have generally taken the view that the death of a defendant at any time prior to the determination of his or her final direct appeal abates all underlying proceedings; appeals are dismissed as moot, convictions are overturned, indictments are dismissed, and abated convictions cannot be used in related civil litigation against the estate — all as if the defendant was never criminally charged.[168] It might seem from this that a restitution order would abate as well, but there is no consensus among the lower federal courts on the issue.[169]

APPENDIX: STATUTORY TEXT

18 U.S.C. 3663. Order of restitution

(a)(1)(A) The court, when sentencing a defendant convicted of an offense under this title, Section 401, 408(a), 409, 416, 420, or 422(a) of the Controlled Substances Act (21 U.S.C. 841, 848(a), 849, 856, 861, 863) (but in no case shall a participant in an offense under such sections be considered a victim of such offense under this section), or Section 5124, 46312, 46502, or 46504 of Title 49, other than an offense described in Section 3663A(c), may order, in addition to or, in the case of a misdemeanor, in lieu of any other penalty authorized by law, that the defendant make restitution to any victim of such offense, or if the victim is deceased, to the victim's estate. The court may also order, if agreed to by the parties in a plea agreement, restitution to persons other than the victim of the offense.

(B)(i) The court, in determining whether to order restitution under this section, shall consider — (I) the amount of the loss sustained by each victim as a result of the offense; and (II) the financial resources of the defendant, the financial needs and earning ability of the defendant and the defendant's dependents, and such other factors as the court deems appropriate.

(ii) To the extent that the court determines that the complication and prolongation of the sentencing process resulting from the fashioning of an order of restitution under this section outweighs the need to provide restitution to any victims, the court may decline to make such an order.

(2) For the purposes of this section, the term "victim" means a person directly and proximately harmed as a result of the commission of an offense for which restitution may be ordered including, in the case of an offense that involves as an element a scheme, conspiracy, or pattern of criminal activity, any person directly harmed by the defendant's criminal conduct in the course of the scheme, conspiracy, or pattern. In the case of a victim who is under 18 years of age, incompetent, incapacitated, or deceased, the legal guardian of the victim or representative of the victim's estate, another family member, or any other person appointed as suitable by the court, may assume the victim's rights under this section, but in no event shall the defendant be named as such representative or guardian.

(3) The court may also order restitution in any criminal case to the extent agreed to by the parties in a plea agreement.

(b) The order may require that such defendant —

(1) in the case of an offense resulting in damage to or loss or destruction of property of a victim of the offense —

(A) return the property to the owner of the property or someone designated by the owner; or

(B) if return of the property under subparagraph (A) is impossible, impractical, or inadequate, pay an amount equal to the greater of —

(i) the value of the property on the date of the damage, loss, or destruction, or

(ii) the value of the property on the date of sentencing, less the value (as of the date the property is returned) of any part of the property that is returned;

(2) in the case of an offense resulting in bodily injury to a victim including an offense under chapter 109A or chapter 110 —

(A) pay an amount equal to the cost of necessary medical and related professional services and devices relating to physical, psychiatric, and psychological care, including nonmedical care and treatment rendered in accordance with a method of healing recognized by the law of the place of treatment;

(B) pay an amount equal to the cost of necessary physical and occupational therapy and rehabilitation; and

(C) reimburse the victim for income lost by such victim as a result of such offense;

(3) in the case of an offense resulting in bodily injury also results in the death of a victim, pay an amount equal to the cost of necessary funeral and related services;

(4) in any case, reimburse the victim for lost income and necessary child care, transportation, and other expenses related to participation in the investigation or prosecution of the offense or attendance at proceedings related to the offense; and

(5) in any case, if the victim (or if the victim is deceased, the victim's estate) consents, make restitution in services in lieu of money, or make restitution to a person or organization designated by the victim or the estate.

(c)(1) Notwithstanding any other provision of law (but subject to the provisions of subsections (a)(1)(B)(i)(II) and (ii), [FN1] when sentencing a defendant convicted of an offense described in Section 401, 408(a), 409, 416, 420, or 422(a) of the Controlled Substances Act (21 U.S.C. 841, 848(a), 849, 856, 861, 863), in which there is no identifiable victim, the court may order that the defendant make restitution in accordance with this subsection.

(2)(A) An order of restitution under this subsection shall be based on the amount of public harm caused by the offense, as determined by the court in accordance with guidelines promulgated by the United States Sentencing Commission.

(B) In no case shall the amount of restitution ordered under this subsection exceed the amount of the fine which may be ordered for the offense charged in the case.

(3) Restitution under this subsection shall be distributed as follows:

(A) 65 percent of the total amount of restitution shall be paid to the State entity designated to administer crime victim assistance in the State in which the crime occurred.

(B) 35 percent of the total amount of restitution shall be paid to the State entity designated to receive Federal substance abuse block grant funds.

(4) The court shall not make an award under this subsection if it appears likely that such award would interfere with a forfeiture under chapter 46 or chapter 96 of this title or under the Controlled Substances Act (21 U.S.C. 801 et seq.).

(5) Notwithstanding Section 3612(c) or any other provision of law, a penalty assessment under Section 3013 or a fine under subchapter C of chapter 227 shall take precedence over an order of restitution under this subsection.

(6) Requests for community restitution under this subsection may be considered in all plea agreements negotiated by the United States.

(7)(A) The United States Sentencing Commission shall promulgate guidelines to assist courts in determining the amount of restitution that may be ordered under this subsection.

(B) No restitution shall be ordered under this subsection until such time as the Sentencing Commission promulgates guidelines pursuant to this paragraph.

(d) An order of restitution made pursuant to this section shall be issued and enforced in accordance with Section 3664.

18 U.S.C. 3663A. Mandatory restitution

(a)(1) Notwithstanding any other provision of law, when sentencing a defendant convicted of an offense described in subsection (c), the court shall order, in addition to, or in the case of a misdemeanor, in addition to or in lieu of, any other penalty authorized by law, that the defendant make restitution to the victim of the offense or, if the victim is deceased, to the victim's estate.

(2) For the purposes of this section, the term "victim" means a person directly and proximately harmed as a result of the commission of an offense for which restitution may be ordered including, in the case of an offense that involves as an element a scheme, conspiracy, or pattern of criminal activity, any person directly harmed by the defendant's criminal conduct in the course of the scheme, conspiracy, or pattern. In the case of a victim who is under 18 years of age, incompetent, incapacitated, or deceased, the legal guardian of the victim or representative of the victim's estate, another family member, or

any other person appointed as suitable by the court, may assume the victim's rights under this section, but in no event shall the defendant be named as such representative or guardian.

(3) The court shall also order, if agreed to by the parties in a plea agreement, restitution to persons other than the victim of the offense.

(b) The order of restitution shall require that such defendant —

(1) in the case of an offense resulting in damage to or loss or destruction of property of a victim of the offense — (A) return the property to the owner of the property or someone designated by the owner; or (B) if return of the property under subparagraph (A) is impossible, impracticable, or inadequate, pay an amount equal to — (i) the greater of — (I) the value of the property on the date of the damage, loss, or destruction; or (II) the value of the property on the date of sentencing, less (ii) the value (as of the date the property is returned) of any part of the property that is returned; (2) in the case of an offense resulting in bodily injury to a victim — (A) pay an amount equal to the cost of necessary medical and related professional services and devices relating to physical, psychiatric, and psychological care, including nonmedical care and treatment rendered in accordance with a method of healing recognized by the law of the place of treatment; (B) pay an amount equal to the cost of necessary physical and occupational therapy and rehabilitation; and (C) reimburse the victim for income lost by such victim as a result of such offense; (3) in the case of an offense resulting in bodily injury that results in the death of the victim, pay an amount equal to the cost of necessary funeral and related services; and (4) in any case, reimburse the victim for lost income and necessary child care, transportation, and other expenses incurred during participation in the investigation or prosecution of the offense or attendance at proceedings related to the offense.

(c)(1) This section shall apply in all sentencing proceedings for convictions of, or plea agreements relating to charges for, any offense — (A) that is — (i) a crime of violence, as defined in Section 16; (ii) an offense against property under this title, or under Section 416(a) of the Controlled Substances Act (21 U.S.C. 856(a)), including any offense committed by fraud or deceit; or (iii) an offense described in Section 1365 (relating to tampering with consumer products); and (B) in which an identifiable victim or victims has suffered a physical injury or pecuniary loss.

(2) In the case of a plea agreement that does not result in a conviction for an offense described in paragraph (1), this section shall apply only if the plea specifically states that an offense listed under such paragraph gave rise to the plea agreement.

(3) This section shall not apply in the case of an offense described in paragraph (1)(A)(ii) if the court finds, from facts on the record, that — (A) the number of identifiable victims is so large as to make restitution impracticable; or (B) determining complex issues of fact related to the cause or amount of the victim's losses would complicate or prolong the sentencing process to a degree that the need to provide restitution to any victim is outweighed by the burden on the sentencing process.

(d) An order of restitution under this section shall be issued and enforced in accordance with Section 3664.

18 U.S.C. 3664. Procedure

(a) For orders of restitution under this title, the court shall order the probation officer to obtain and include in its presentence report, or in a separate report, as the court may direct, information sufficient for the court to exercise its discretion in fashioning a restitution order. The report shall include, to the extent practicable, a complete accounting of the losses to each victim, any restitution owed pursuant to a plea agreement, and information relating to the economic circumstances of each defendant. If the number or identity of victims cannot be reasonably ascertained, or other circumstances exist that make this requirement clearly impracticable, the probation officer shall so inform the court.

(b) The court shall disclose to both the defendant and the attorney for the Government all portions of the presentence or other report pertaining to the matters described in subsection (a) of this section.

(c) The provisions of this chapter, chapter 227, and Rule 32(c) of the Federal Rules of Criminal Procedure shall be the only rules applicable to proceedings under this section.

(d)(1) Upon the request of the probation officer, but not later than 60 days prior to the date initially set for sentencing, the attorney for the Government, after consulting, to the extent practicable, with all identified victims, shall promptly provide the probation officer with a listing of the amounts subject to restitution.

(2) The probation officer shall, prior to submitting the presentence report under subsection (a), to the extent practicable — (A) provide notice to all identified victims of — (i) the offense or offenses of which the defendant was convicted; (ii) the amounts subject to restitution submitted to the probation officer; (iii) the opportunity of the victim to submit information to the probation officer concerning the amount of the victim's losses; (iv) the

scheduled date, time, and place of the sentencing hearing; (v) the availability of a lien in favor of the victim pursuant to subsection (m)(1)(B); and (vi) the opportunity of the victim to file with the probation officer a separate affidavit relating to the amount of the victim's losses subject to restitution; and (B) provide the victim with an affidavit form to submit pursuant to subparagraph (A)(vi).

(3) Each defendant shall prepare and file with the probation officer an affidavit fully describing the financial resources of the defendant, including a complete listing of all assets owned or controlled by the defendant as of the date on which the defendant was arrested, the financial needs and earning ability of the defendant and the defendant's dependents, and such other information that the court requires relating to such other factors as the court deems appropriate.

(4) After reviewing the report of the probation officer, the court may require additional documentation or hear testimony. The privacy of any records filed, or testimony heard, pursuant to this section shall be maintained to the greatest extent possible, and such records may be filed or testimony heard in camera.

(5) If the victim's losses are not ascertainable by the date that is 10 days prior to sentencing, the attorney for the Government or the probation officer shall so inform the court, and the court shall set a date for the final determination of the victim's losses, not to exceed 90 days after sentencing. If the victim subsequently discovers further losses, the victim shall have 60 days after discovery of those losses in which to petition the court for an amended restitution order. Such order may be granted only upon a showing of good cause for the failure to include such losses in the initial claim for restitutionary relief.

(6) The court may refer any issue arising in connection with a proposed order of restitution to a magistrate judge or special master for proposed findings of fact and recommendations as to disposition, subject to a de novo determination of the issue by the court.

(e) Any dispute as to the proper amount or type of restitution shall be resolved by the court by the preponderance of the evidence. The burden of demonstrating the amount of the loss sustained by a victim as a result of the offense shall be on the attorney for the Government. The burden of demonstrating the financial resources of the defendant and the financial needs of the defendant's dependents, shall be on the defendant. The burden of demonstrating such other matters as the court deems appropriate shall be upon the party designated by the court as justice requires.

(f)(1)(A) In each order of restitution, the court shall order restitution to each victim in the full amount of each victim's losses as determined by the court and without consideration of the economic circumstances of the defendant.

(B) In no case shall the fact that a victim has received or is entitled to receive compensation with respect to a loss from insurance or any other source be considered in determining the amount of restitution.

(2) Upon determination of the amount of restitution owed to each victim, the court shall, pursuant to Section 3572, specify in the restitution order the manner in which, and the schedule according to which, the restitution is to be paid, in consideration of — (A) the financial resources and other assets of the defendant, including whether any of these assets are jointly controlled; (B) projected earnings and other income of the defendant; and (C) any financial obligations of the defendant; including obligations to dependents.

(3)(A) A restitution order may direct the defendant to make a single, lump-sum payment, partial payments at specified intervals, in-kind payments, or a combination of payments at specified intervals and in-kind payments.

(B) A restitution order may direct the defendant to make nominal periodic payments if the court finds from facts on the record that the economic circumstances of the defendant do not allow the payment of any amount of a restitution order, and do not allow for the payment of the full amount of a restitution order in the foreseeable future under any reasonable schedule of payments.

(4) An in-kind payment described in paragraph (3) may be in the form of — (A) return of property; (B) replacement of property; or (C) if the victim agrees, services rendered to the victim or a person or organization other than the victim.

(g)(1) No victim shall be required to participate in any phase of a restitution order.

(2) A victim may at any time assign the victim's interest in restitution payments to the Crime Victims Fund in the Treasury without in any way impairing the obligation of the defendant to make such payments.

(h) If the court finds that more than 1 defendant has contributed to the loss of a victim, the court may make each defendant liable for payment of the full amount of restitution or may apportion liability among the defendants to reflect the level of contribution to the victim's loss and economic circumstances of each defendant.

(i) If the court finds that more than 1 victim has sustained a loss requiring restitution by a defendant, the court may provide for a different payment schedule for each victim based on the type and amount of each victim's loss and accounting for the economic circumstances of each victim. In any case in which the United States is a victim, the court shall ensure that all other victims receive full restitution before the United States receives any restitution.

(j)(1) If a victim has received compensation from insurance or any other source with respect to a loss, the court shall order that restitution be paid to the person who provided or is obligated to provide the compensation, but the restitution order shall provide that all restitution of victims required by the order be paid to the victims before any restitution is paid to such a provider of compensation.

(2) Any amount paid to a victim under an order of restitution shall be reduced by any amount later recovered as compensatory damages for the same loss by the victim in — (A) any Federal civil proceeding; and (B) any State civil proceeding, to the extent provided by the law of the State.

(k) A restitution order shall provide that the defendant shall notify the court and the Attorney General of any material change in the defendant's economic circumstances that might affect the defendant's ability to pay restitution. The court may also accept notification of a material change in the defendant's economic circumstances from the United States or from the victim. The Attorney General shall certify to the court that the victim or victims owed restitution by the defendant have been notified of the change in circumstances. Upon receipt of the notification, the court may, on its own motion, or the motion of any party, including the victim, adjust the payment schedule, or require immediate payment in full, as the interests of justice require.

(l) A conviction of a defendant for an offense involving the act giving rise to an order of restitution shall estop the defendant from denying the essential allegations of that offense in any subsequent Federal civil proceeding or State civil proceeding, to the extent consistent with State law, brought by the victim.

(m)(1)(A)(i) An order of restitution may be enforced by the United States in the manner provided for in subchapter C of chapter 227 and subchapter B of chapter 229 of this title; or (ii) by all other available and reasonable means.

(B) At the request of a victim named in a restitution order, the clerk of the court shall issue an abstract of judgment certifying that a judgment has been entered in favor of such victim in the amount specified in the restitution order. Upon registering, recording, docketing, or indexing such abstract in accordance with the rules and requirements relating to judgments of the court of the State where the district court is located, the abstract of judgment shall be a lien on the property of the defendant located in such State in the same manner and to the same extent and under the same conditions as a judgment of a court of general jurisdiction in that State.

(2) An order of in-kind restitution in the form of services shall be enforced by the probation officer.

(n) If a person obligated to provide restitution, or pay a fine, receives substantial resources from any source, including inheritance, settlement, or other judgment, during a period of incarceration, such person shall be required to apply the value of such resources to any restitution or fine still owed.

(o) A sentence that imposes an order of restitution is a final judgment notwithstanding the fact that — (1) such a sentence can subsequently be — (A) corrected under Rule 35 of the Federal Rules of Criminal Procedure and Section 3742 of chapter 235 of this title; (B) appealed and modified under Section 3742; (C) amended under subsection (d)(5); or (D) adjusted under Section 3664(k), 3572, or 3613A; or (2) the defendant may be resentenced under Section 3565 or 3614.

(p) Nothing in this section or sections 2248, 2259, 2264, 2327, 3663, and 3663A and arising out of the application of such sections, shall be construed to create a cause of action not otherwise authorized in favor of any person against the United States or any officer or employee of the United States.

REFERENCES

[1] *United States v. Gordon*, 480 F.3d 1205, 1210 (10th Cir. 2007); *United States v. Reifler*, 446 F.3d 65, 127 (2d Cir. 2006); *United States v. Love*, 431 F.3d 477, 479 (5th Cir. 2005); *United States v. Rand*, 403 F.3d 489, 493 (7th Cir. 2005).

[2] 18 U.S.C. 3663A(a), (c).

[3] Id.

[4] 21 U.S.C. 856; 18 U.S.C. 3663A(a), (c).

[5] 18 U.S.C. 43(c).

[6] 18 U.S.C. 228(d).

[7] 18 U.S.C. 1593.

[8] 18 U.S.C. 2248.

[9] 18 U.S.C. 2259.

[10] 18 U.S.C. 2264.

[11] 18 U.S.C. 2327.

[12] 21 U.S.C. 853(q).

[13] 18 U.S.C. 3664(f).

[14] *United States v. Roper*, 462 F.3d 336, 337-40 (4th Cir. 2006).

[15] 18 U.S.C. 3663A(b). A defendant may agree in a plea bargain to pay restitution to an extent not otherwise authorized, 18 U.S.C. 3663(a)(3); *United States v. Fariduddin*, 469 F.3d 1111, 1111 (7th Cir. 2006)(a defendant may waive protections afforded him under the federal restitution laws).

[16] 18 U.S.C. 3663.

[17] 18 U.S.C. 3563(b)(2), 3583(d).

[18] "[A]lthough restitution of property obtained under a contract which was illegal, because *ultra vires*, cannot be adjudged by force of the illegal contract, yet, as the obligation to do justice rests upon all persons, natural and artificial, if one obtains the money or property of others without authority, the law, independently of express contract, will compel restitution or compensation," *Rankin v. Emigh*, 218 U.S. 27, 35 (1910).

[19] "'Equitable relief' can also refer to those categories of relief that were typically available in equity (such as injunction, mandamus, and *restitution*, but not compensatory damages)," *Mertens v. Hewitt Associates*, 508 U.S. 248, 256 (1993)(emphasis added); see also, Seavey, *Problems in Restitution*, 7 OKLAHOMA LAW REVIEW 257, 257 (1954)("Restitution is the equitable principle by which one who has been enriched at the expense of another, whether by mistake, or otherwise, is under a duty to return what he has received or its value to the other").

[20] Murphy, *Misclassifying Monetary Restitution*, 55 SMU LAW REVIEW 1577, 1598-1607 (2002); IV BLACKSTONE, COMMENTARIES ON THE LAWS OF ENGLAND 356 (1769) (transliteration supplied)("[I]f any person be convicted of larciny by the evidence of the party robbed, he shall have full restitution of his money, goods, and chattels, or the value of them out of the offender's goods, if [he] has any, by the writ to be granted by the justices. And this writ of restitution shall reach the goods so stolen, notwithstanding the property of them is endeavoured to be altered by sale in market overt").

[21] *Firefighters v. Stotts*, 467 U.S. 561, 582 n.15 (1984)("federal courts are empowered to fashion such relief as the particular circumstances of a

case may require to effect restitution, making whole insofar as possible the victim....”); *United States v. Hudson*, 483 F.3d 707, (10th Cir. 2007)(“The purpose of restitution is ... to ensure that victims, to the greatest extent possible, are made whole for their losses”).

[22] H.Rept. 68-1377 at 3 (1925)(“[T]he United States district courts suspended sentence in many instances, and certain courts used a form of probation, though without legislative authority, placing defendant under the supervision of state probation officers or volunteers.” State probation officers worked under systems in which “greatly increased sums [were] collected for fines, restitution, and especially family support”).

[23] *Ex parte United States*, 242 U.S. 27, 51-2 (1916).

[24] P.L. 68-596, 43 Stat. 1259 (1925).

[25] 43 Stat. at 1260.

[26] 18 U.S.C. 3651 (1976 ed.)(“While on probation and among the conditions thereof, the defendant — May be required to pay a fine in one or several sums; and May be required to make restitution or reparation to the aggrieved party or parties for actual damages or loss caused by the offense for which conviction was had, and May be required to provide for the support of any persons for whose support he is legally responsible).

[27] *United States v. Elkins*, 731 F.2d 1005, 1010-11 (2d Cir. 1984)(a federal court has no inherent power to order restitution; the authority must be found in statute); S.Rept. 97-532, at 30 (1982)(“Current law does not contain a provision covering an order of restitution as a part of any sentence other than probation”).

[28] Id.

[29] “Crime victims and their advocates have called on state legislators to restore restitution to its proper place in criminal law. They point out that the average dollar losses victims suffer total hundreds of dollars, not thousands, and that most ex-offenders, not just those on probation , have some means to undo the financial harm they have done. There is no reason to believe that victims of federal crimes do not have the same grievances,” id.

[30] P.L. 97-291, 96 Stat. 1253 (1982); now found as amended at 18 U.S.C. 3663.

[31] P.L. 103-322, 108 Stat. 1904, 1906, 1928 (1994), 18 U.S.C. 2248, 2259, and 2264, respectively.

[32] P.L. 104-132, 110 Stat. 1227 (1996), 18 U.S.C. 3663A.

[33] *Tull v. United States*, 481 U.S. 412, 417-18 (1987)

[34] *United States v. Florence*, 741 F.2d 1066, 1067-68 (8th Cir. 1984); *United States v. Statterfield*, 743 F.2d 827, 836-37 (11th Cir. 1984); *United States v. Brown*, 744 F.2d 905, 910-11 (2d Cir. 1984); *United States v. Keith*, 754 F.2d 1388, 1391-392 (9th Cir. 1985); *United States v. Watchman*, 749 F.2d 616, 617 (10th Cir. 1984); *United States v. Palma*, 760 F.2d 475, 479-80 (3d Cir. 1985); *United States v. Gomer*, 764 F.2d 1221, 1228-229 (7th Cir. 1985).

[35] *United States v. Leahy*, 438 F.3d 328, 335 (3d Cir. 2006)(ex post facto clause applies); *accord*, *United States v. Grice*, 319 F.3d 1174, 1177 (9th Cir. 2003); *United States v. Schulte*, 264 F.3d 656, 662 (6th Cir. 2001); *United States v. Siegel*, 153 F.3d 1256, 1260 (11th Cir. 1998); *United States v. Bapack*, 129 F.3d 1320, 1327 n.13 (D.C. Cir. 1997); *United States v. Williams*, 128 F.3d 1239, 1241 (8th Cir. 1997); *United States v. Thompson*, 113 F.3d 13, 15, n.1 (2d Cir. 1997); *United States v. Rico Industries, Inc.*, 854 F.2d 710, 714 (5th Cir. 1988); *contra*, *United States v. Baldwin*, 414 F.3d 791, 800 (7th Cir. 2005); *United States v. Nichols*, 169 F.3d 1255, 1279-280 (10th Cir. 1999).

[36] *United States v. Newsome*, 322 F.3d 328, 342 (4th Cir. 2003); *United States v. Dubose*, 146 F.3d 1141, 1148 (9th Cir. 1998).

[37] *United States v. Bajakajian*, 524 U.S. 321, 337 (1998)("If the amount of the forfeiture is grossly disproportional to the gravity of the defendant's offense, it is unconstitutional" under the excessive fines clause); *cf.*, *Lockyer v. Andrade*, 538 U.S. 63, 72 (2003)(noting that for purposes of the cruel and unusual punishments clause, the "gross disproportionality principle" is the appropriate standard but that the factors that evidence such imbalance are less easily identified).

[38] *United States v. Beydoun*, 469 F.3d 102, 107 (5th Cir. 2006); *United States v. Boccagna*, 450 F.3d 107, 117 (2d Cir. 2006); *United States v. Gordon*, 393 F.3d 1044, 1060 (9th Cir. 2004); *United States v. Dawson*, 250 F.3d 1048, 1050 (7th Cir. 2001).

[39] 530 U.S. 466 (2000).

[40] 543 U.S. 220 (2005).

[41] *United States v. Booker*, 543 U.S. at 244; *see also*, *Apprendi v. New Jersey*, 530 U.S. at 490.

[42] *United States v. Oslund*, 453 F.3d 1048, 1062 (8th Cir. 2006); *United States v. Reifler*, 446 F.3d 65, 118 (2d Cir. 2006); *United States v. Leahy*, 438 F.3d 328, 331 (3d Cir. 2006); *United States v. Belk*, 435 F.3d 817, 819 (7th Cir. 2006); *United States v. Garza*, 429 F.3d 165, 170 (5th Cir. 2005); *United States v. Visinaiz*, 428 F.3d 1300, 1316 (10th Cir,. 2005); *United States v. Sosebee*, 419 F.3d 451, 461 (6th Cir.

2005); *United States v. Antonakopoulous*, 399 F.3d 68, 83 (1st Cir. 2005). Cases reaching the same conclusion but decided between *Apprendi* and *Booker* include *United States v. DeGeorge*, 380 F.3d 1203, 1221 (9th Cir. 2004); *United States v. Wooten*, 377 F.3d 1134, 1144-145 (10th Cir. 2004).

[43] *United States v. Veerapol*, 312 ?F.3d 1128, 1134 (9th Cir. 2002)(the procedure afforded the defendant notice and opportunity to contest sufficient to satisfy due process); *United States v. Dubose*, 146 F.3d 1141, 1147 (9th Cir. 1998)(no due process or equal protection infirmity); *United States v. Craig*, 181 F.3d 1124, (9th Cir. 1999)(notice sufficient to satisfy due process); *United States v. Smith*, 944 F.2d 618, (9th Cir. 1991)(restitution procedure, which afforded the defendant fewer discovery options than he would have enjoyed had the victim brought a civil action on the same grounds, did not offend due process); *United States v. Gomer*, 764 F.2d 1221, 1229 (7th Cir. 1985)(defendant received adequate notice and opportunity to contest); *United States v. Palma*, 760 F.2d 475, 477-79 (3d Cir. 1985) (restitution procedure met the demands of due process and equal protection); *United States v. Keith*, 754 F.2d 1388, 1392 (9th Cir. 1985) (no due process violation in light of defendant's opportunity to contest); *United States v. Florence*, 741 F.2d 1066, 1068-69 (8th Cir. 1984) (sentencing hearing evidentiary standards satisfied due process).

[44] 18 U.S.C. 3579 (1982 ed.). The original section was redesignated as 18 U.S.C. 3663 as part of the 1984 Sentencing Reform Act, P.L. 98-473, 98 Stat. 2010 (1984).

[45] *Hughey v. United States*, 495 U.S. 411, 422 (1990). Hughey was originally charged with several counts of credit card fraud. He pleaded guilty to a single count, but the trial court ordered restitution to the issuing bank for losses identified in the counts that had been dropped as part of the plea agreement. The Court disagreed, "The plain language of VWPA makes clear that the District Court's restitution order in this case was unauthorized. Petitioner pleaded guilty only the charge that he fraudulently used the credit card of Hershey Godfrey. Because the restitution order encompassed losses stemming from alleged fraudulent uses of cards issued to persons other than Godfrey, such portions of the order are invalid," *id.*

[46] P.L. 101-647, 104 Stat. 4863, 4931 (1990), 18 U.S.C. 3663(a)(2) (1988 ed. and Supp. II).

[47] P.L. 104-132, 110 Stat. 1227, 1229 (1996), 18 U.S.C. 3663(a)(2), 3663A(a)(2)(1994 ed. and Supp. II).

[48] 18 U.S.C. 3663(a)(1)(A) ("... that the defendant make restitution to any victim of such offense, or if the victim is deceased, to the victim's estate...."); 3663A(a)(1) ("... that the defendant make restitution to any victim of the offense, or if the victim is deceased, to the victim's estate.").

[49] 18 U.S.C. 3663(a)(2)("... in the case of an offense that involves as an element a scheme, conspiracy, or patter of criminal activity, any person directly harmed by the defendant's criminal conduct in the course of the scheme, conspiracy, or pattern...."); 3663A(a)(2)(same).

[50] The apparent duplication arises when the victim is deceased. The first instance permits an order of restitution to the victim's estate if the victim is deceased, 18 U.S.C. 3663(a)(1)(A) ("... that the defendant make restitution to any victim of such offense, or if the victim is deceased, to the victim's estate...."); 3663A(a)(1) (same). The second permits orders for the representatives of the deceased and of underaged or incapacitated victims as well, 3663(a)(2)("... In the case of a victim who is under 18 years of age, incompetent, incapacitated, or deceased, the legal guardian of the victim or representative of the victim's estate, another family member, or any other person appointed as suitable by the court, may assume the victim's rights under this section, but in no event shall the defendant be named as such representative or guardian"); 3663A(a)(2)(same).

[51] 18 U.S.C. 3663(a)(1)(A)("... The court may also order, if agreed to by the parties in a plea agreement, restitution to persons other than the victims of the offense"); 3663A(a)(2) ("The court shall also order, if agreed to by the parties in a plea agreement, restitution to persons other than the victims of the offense").

[52] Under the Dictionary Act, "[i]n determining the meaning of any Act of Congress, *unless the context indicates otherwise* ... the words 'person' and 'whoever' include corporations, companies, associations, firms, partnerships, associations , and joint stock companies, as well as individuals," 1 U.S.C. 1 (emphasis added); *see also*, *United States v. United Mine Workers*, 330 U.S. 258m, 275 (1947)("The Act does not define 'persons.' In common usage that term does not include the sovereign, and statutes employing it will ordinarily not be construed to do so"). Of course, human beings are persons even when victimized while acting in an official capacity, *United States v. Holthaus*, 486 F.3d 451, 458 (8th Cir. 2007)(finding that "bankruptcy trustees qualify as victims under the statute if their compensation is negatively impacted by a debtor's misrepresentation," after the defendant argued

that trustees could not be considered "persons" for restitution purposes).

[53] *United States v. Mickle*, 464 F.3d 804, 810-11 (8th Cir. 2006) (Minnesota); *United States v. Leahy*, 464 F.3d 773, 793 (7th Cir. 2007)(Chicago); *United States v. Woodard*, 459 F.3d 1078, 1087-88 (11th Cir. 2006)(Atlanta); *United States v. Senty-Haugen*, 449 F.3d 862, 865 (8th Cir. 2006)(U.S. Internal Revenue Service); *United States v. Washington* , 434 F.3d 1265, (11th Cir. 2006)(Ormond Beach police department); *United States v. Ekanem*, 383 F.3d 40, 42-3 (2d Cir. 2004)(U.S. Department of Agriculture); *United States v. Phillips*, 367 F.3d 846, 862-64 (9th Cir. 2004)(U.S. Government); *United States v. Vaknin*, 112 F.3d 579, 591 (1st Cir. 1997)(Federal Deposit Insurance Corp.). In a fraud case, restitution to the government should be set at the amount the government "paid minus the amount that would have been paid in the absence of fraud," *United States v. Petruk*, 484 F.3d 1035, 1038 (8th Cir. 2007); *United States v. Leahy*, 464 F.3d 773, 794 (7th Cir. 2006).

[54] 18 U.S.C. 3663(a)(2), 3663A(a)(2).

[55] *United States v. Wilcox*, 487 F.3d 1163, 1176-178 (8th Cir. 2007)(restitution may not include income lost by the mother of a rape victim under the theory that the child's mother was likewise a victim of the crime, but may include reimbursement to the mother for the cost of transporting the child to receive crime-necessitated medical treatment); *United States v. Hayward*, 359 F.3d 631, 642 (3d Cir. 2004)(upholding a restitution order for the parents whose children had been transported to London for illicit sexual purposes with the terse observation that the parents "incurred reasonable costs in obtaining the return of their victimized children from London and in making their children available to participate in the investigation and trial. The restitution order will therefore be affirmed").

[56] 18 U.S.C. 3663(a)(2), 3663A(a)(2).

[57] *United States v. Cutter*, 313 F.3d 1, 7 (1st Cir. 2002); *United States v. LaFuente*, 353 F.3d 766, 772 (9th Cir. 2003)("The main inquiry for causation in investigation cases is whether there was an intervening cause, and if so, whether this intervening cause was directly related to the offense. [The] Defendant's conduct need not be the sole cause of the loss, but any subsequent action that contributes to the loss such as an intervening cause must be directly related to the defendant's conduct. We have approved restitution awards that included losses at least one step removed from the offense conduct itself, but the causal

chain may not extend so far, in terms of the facts or the time span, as to become unreasonable")(internal citations and quotation marks omitted). *See also*, *United States v. Gamma Tech Industries, Inc.*, 265 F.3d 917, 927-28 (9th Cir. 2001)("In several cases, we have concluded that losses did not result directly from a defendant's criminal conduct, because either there was an unrelated, intervening cause, or the criminal conduct to which a defendant pleaded guilty did not cause the loss. *See e.g.*, *United States v. Meksian,* 170 F.3d 1260, 1263 (9th Cir. 1999)(rejecting mere 'but for' standard for proving loss and reversing restitution order in fraudulent loan application case because an intervening cause for the erroneous issuance of the loan, an inaccurate environment report, was not directly related to the offense conduct); *United States v. Sablan*, 92 F.3d 865, 870 (9th Cir. 1996) (reversing restitution order based on consequential damages, such as expenses arising from meetings with law enforcement officers investigating the crime, because such expenses were not necessary to repair damage caused by defendant's criminal conduct); *United States v. Reed*, 80 F.3d 1419, 1421 (9th Cir. 1996)(reversing restitution order based on damage to private vehicles occurring during flight from police where the offense of conviction was illegal possession of a firearm by a felon); *United States v. Tyler*, 767 F.2 1350, 1351 (9th Cir. 1985)(rejecting restitution awarded under then section 3651 because losses based on depressed market prices were too remote). However, we have approved restitution awards that included losses at least one step removed from the offense conduct itself. *See e.g.*, *United States v. Rice*, 38 F.3d 1536, 1542 (9th Cir. 1994)(upholding in conspiracy and mail fraud case, restitution based on the victim's inability to use entire inventory of parts supplied by defendant because victim could not identify which parts were defective); [*United States v.*] *Koenig*, 952 F.2d [267], 274-75 [(9th Cir. 1991)] (upholding, in case involving conspiracy to produce and use counterfeit automated teller machine cards, restitution for the cost of reprogramming bank computers after defendants had stolen ATM account information"); *United States v. Berger*, 473 F.3d 1080, 1107 (9th Cir. 2007); *but see*, *United States v. Sosebee*, 419 F.3d 451, 459 (6th Cir. 2005)(finding that the defendant convicted only of misprision of a felony for failing to report a fraudulent conspiracy was thereby "a direct and proximate cause of some or all of the victim's losses" inflicted by the conspirators and therefore the appropriate subject of a restitution order); *United States v. Fallon*, 470 F.3d 542, 549 (3d Cir. 2005)(where "a business transaction was consummated due to fraud by the defendant, a commonsense, but rebuttable inference arises that subsequent losses suffered by the victim of the fraud are sufficiently linked to the underlying fraud to support an award of restitution").

[58] *United States v. Washington*, 434 F.3d 1265, 1268-270 (11th Cir. 2006); *United States v. Reichow*, 416 F.3d 802, 805 (8th Cir. 2005); *United States v. Donaby*, 349 F.3d 1046, 1053 (7th Cir. 2003).

[59] 18 U.S.C. 3663(a)(2); 3663A(a)(2); *United States v. Napier*, 463 F.3d 1040, 1046 (9th Cir. 2006)("Restitution may go beyond the offense of conviction under certain conditions if the offense of conviction contains an element of a scheme, conspiracy or pattern of criminal activity").

[60] *United States v. Rand*, 403 F.3d 489, 495 (7th Cir. 2005); *United States v. Riley*, 335 F.3d 919, 932 (9th Cir. 2003); *United States v. Solares*, 236 F.3d 24, 26(1st Cir. 2000); *United States v. Osborne*, 332 F.3d 1307, 1314 (10th Cir 2003)("the losses caused by the entire conspiracy, not just the losses caused by those acts committed by the defendant, can be attributed to the defendant when the district court orders restitution"); *but see*, *United States v. Reifler*, 446 F.3d 65, 125-27 (2d Cir. 2006)(a district court had no authority to order restitution to those "victimized" after the indictment was announced nor to coconspirators).

[61] 18 U.S.C. 1341 (mail fraud), 1343 (wire fraud); 18 U.S.C. 1962 (racketeer influenced and corrupt organization (RICO) offenses).

[62] *United States v. Johnson*, 440 F.3d 832, 850 (6th Cir. 2006)("Stone does not dispute that one element of a RICO offense and a RICO conspiracy is a pattern of criminal activity. . . The district court could therefore award restitution to any victim harmed by the defendant's criminal conduct in the course of the RICO activity"); *United States v. Belk*, 435 F.3d 817, 819 (7th Cir. 2006)("The crime covered by §1341is the scheme to defraud, not (just) the mailings that occur in the course of the scheme. This indictment laid out, and the jury convicted Belk of, a multi-year scheme to defraud Rogge's brokerage. The eight mailings [listed in the indictment] were just overt acts. Restitution for the whole scheme is in order"); *United States v. Dickerson*, 370 F.3d 1330, 1342 (11th Cir. 2004) ("Therefore, we hold that where a defendant is convicted of a crime of which a scheme is an element the district court must under 18 U.S.C. 3663A, order the defendant to pay restitution to all victims for the losses they suffered from the defendant's conduct in the course of the scheme even where such

losses were caused by conduct outside of the statute of limitations"); *United States v. Grice*, 319 F.3d 1174, 1177 (9th Cir. 2003)("When a charged crime involves a scheme to defraud, the court can base restitution under the VWPA on related conduct for which the defendant was not convicted"); *United States v. Bright*, 353 F.3d 1114, 1120 (9th Cir. 2004)("Bright similarly pled guilty to multiple counts of mail fraud, thus acknowledging his participation in a scheme to defraud. The district court therefore properly ordered restitution for losses caused by the dismissed conduct related to this scheme"); *but see*, *United States v. Polichemi*, 219 F.3d 698, 714 (7th Cir. 2000)(defendant convicted of a scheme to defraud may nevertheless not be ordered to pay restitution to victims harmed by conduct for which he was acquitted).

[63] *United States v. Hinojosa*, 484 F.3d 337, 343 (5th Cir. 2007)(restitution may not be ordered for the victims of a different scheme); *United States v. Inman*, 411 F.3d 591, 595 (5th Cir. 2005)("Here, Inman's restitution order under the MVRA was based, in part, on transactions that were not alleged in the indictment and occurred over two years before the specified temporal scope of the indictment. Thus, the district court plainly erred"); *United States v. Flaschberger*, 408 F.3d 941, 943 (7th Cir. 2005)("Losses from the years preceding the scheme alleged in the indictment must be subtracted from the [restitution] award").

[64] *United States v. Maturin*, 488 F.3d 657, 661-62 (5th Cir. 2007)(emphasis of the court) ("Both the statutory language of MVA and this court's prior decisions make it plain that a defendant's conviction on one count can support a broad restitution award encompassing additional losses *only* if the count of conviction requires proof of a scheme, conspiracy or pattern of criminal activity as an element"); *United States v. Napier*, 463 F.3d 1040, 1046 (9th Cir. 2006); *United States v. Reynolds*, 432 F.3d 821, 823 (8th Cir. 2005); *United States v. Davenport*, 445 F.3d 366, (4th Cir. 2006)("Davenport pleaded guilty to fraudulent use of an access device in violation of 18 U.S.C.A. 1029(a)(5). The elements of this offense are: (1) an intent to defraud.... Because Davenport's offense does not 'involve[ ] as an element a scheme, conspiracy, or pattern,' the only question is whether the victims identified by the government were 'directly and proximately harmed' by the offense of conviction"); *United States v. Randle*, 324 F.3d 550, 556 (7th Cir. 2003).

[65] *United States v. Oladimeij*, 463 F.2d 152, 159 (2d Cir. 2006)("Section 1029(a)(3) includes as an element that the possession [of stolen credit cards] be 'with intent to defraud.' Intent to defraud is a 'scheme,' as used in §3663A(a)(2)"); *United States v. Osborne*, 332 F.3d 1307, 1314 (10th Cir. 2003) ("Even when a defendant is not formally convicted of conspiracy, a district court may order a restitution amount for the relevant conduct of others that may be attributed to him" (speaking of defendant who as one of a group of defendants pleaded guilty to bank fraud but not conspiracy)).

[66] *United States v. Bonetti*, 277 F.3d 441, 452-52 (4th Cir. 2002).

[67] *United States v. DeLaFuente*, 353 F.3d 766, 770-71 (9th Cir. 2003)(threats); *United States v. Patrick V.*, 359 F.3d 3, 9 (1st Cir. 2004)(arson); *United States v. Juvenile, G.Z.*, 144 F.3d 1148, 1498 (8th Cir. 1998)(burglary).

[68] *United States v. Dorcely*, 454 F.3d 366, 376 (D.C. Cir. 2006).

[69] *Leocal v. Ashcroft*, 543 U.S. 1, 11 (2004).

[70] *United States v. Hull*, 456 F.3d 133, 138-41 (6th Cir. 2006).

[71] *Garcia v. Gonzales*, 455 F.3d 465, 468-69 (4th Cir. 2006).

[72] *United States v. Villegas-Herndandez*, 468 F.3d 874, 878-85 (5th Cir. 2006).

[73] *Brieva-Peraez v. Gonzales*, 482 F.3d 356, 359-60 (5th Cir. 2007).

[74] Most other controlled substance offenses come within the purview of section 3663.

[75] 18 U.S.C. 3663A(c)(1)(A)(ii).

[76] *United States v. Quarrell*, 310 F.3d 664, (10th Cir. 2002)("The Quarrells also argue the MVRA is inapplicable because a violation of ARPA, 16 U.S.C. 470ee, is not an offense 'under this title,' referring to Title 18. However, the Quarrells were also convicted of conspiracy under 18 U.S.C. 371, which is an offense under Title 18. The Quarrells' conspiracy conviction satisfied the 'under this title' requirement of the MVRA"); *accord*, *United States v. Minneman*, 143 F.3d 274, 284 (7th Cir. 1998); *United States v. Helmsley*, 941 F.2d 71, 101 (2d Cir. 1991).

[77] 18 U.S.C. 3663A(c)(1)(B). Victim identification is a prerequisite to a mandatory restitution order under section 3663A, *United States v. Doe*, 374 F.3d 851, 854 (9th Cir. 2004); *United States v. Zakhary*, 357 F.3d 186, 190 (2d Cir. 2004).

[78] The number of victims and complexity of restitution limitations are only available to defendants convicted of property damage/fraud predicate offenses; they are not available to other defendants subject to

mandatory restitution under section 3663A, *United States v. Cienfuegos*, 462 F.3d 1160, 1168 (9th Cir. 2006).

[79] 18 U.S.C. 3663A(c)(3)(A)("This section shall not apply in the case of an offense described in paragraph (1)(A)(ii) if the court finds, from facts on the record, that — (A) the number of identifiable victims is so large as to make restitution impracticable"). This does not necessarily mean that restitution is barred for identifiable victims simply because other victims may be unidentifiable, *United States v. Grimes*, 173 F.3d 634, 639 (7th Cir. 1999).

[80] 18 U.S.C. 3663A(c)(3)(B)("This section shall not apply in the case of an offense described in paragraph (1)(A)(ii) if the court finds, from facts on the record, that . . .(B) determining complex issues of fact related to the cause or amount of the victim's losses would complicate or prolong the sentencing process to a degree that the need to provide restitution to any victim is outweighed by the burden on the sentencing process."). There is some indication that this exception must be raised either in the presentence report or by the defendant and cannot be asserted by the sentencing court sua sponte, *United States v. Barton*, 366 F.3d 1160, 1166 (10th Cir. 2004).

[81] 18 U.S.C. 3663(a)(1)(A).

[82] Id. The specific controlled substance and air piracy predicates include 21 U.S.C. 841 (trafficking), 848(a) (continuing criminal enterprises), 849 (trafficking at truck stops), 856 (maintaining a place where controlled substances are manufactured, stored, or used), 861(using a child in a trafficking enterprise), 863 (trafficking in drug paraphernalia); and 49 U.S.C. 5124 (tampering with the labeling on hazardous cargo), 46312 (unlawfully transporting hazardous material), 46502 (air piracy), and 46504 (interfering with a flight crew).

[83] 18 U.S.C. 3563(b)(2)("The court may provide,. As further conditions of a sentence of probation ... that the defendant ... (2) make restitution to a victim of the offense under section 3556 (but not subject to the limitation of section 3663(a) or 3663A(c)(1)(A) [which limit the crimes covered by sections 3663 and 3663A]"). Probation is a sentencing option following conviction for any federal crime other than a crime for which probation is specifically prohibited or other than any class A or class B felony (i.e., any federal crime that has a maximum penalty of less than 25 years), 18 U.S.C. 3561(a), 3581. The once-mandatory and now advisory Sentencing Guidelines, however, limit probation to crimes having a sentencing range of 6 to 12 months or less, U.S.S.G. §5B1.1(a), ch.5A (Sentencing Table).

[84] 18 U.S.C. 3583(d)("The court may order, as a further condition of supervised release . . . any condition set forth as a discretionary condition of probation in section 3563(b)(1) through (b)(10). . ."). The court may impose a term supervised release with respect to any federal crime for which it imposes a term of imprisonment, 18 U.S.C. 3583.

[85] *United States v. Love*, 431 F.3d 477, 479-80 (5th Cir. 2005); *United States v. Butler*, 297 F.3d 505, 518 (6th Cir. 2002); *United States v. Frith*, 461 F.3d 914, 919-21 (7th Cir. 2006)(restitution, however, must be limited to losses directly caused by the offense of conviction); *but see*, *United States v. Cottman*, 142 F.3d 160, 169-70 (3d Cir. 1998)(a defendant cannot be ordered to pay restitution for the money used in a government sting since the sting money was a cost of investigation and not a property loss; as a consequence the government cannot be considered a "victim" for purposes of the VWPA under such circumstances); *United States v. Cook*, 406 F.3d 485, 489 (7th Cir. 2005)(return of the government's sting money is more appropriately accomplished as a condition of supervised release); *cf.*, *United States v. Bevilacqua*,447 F.3d 124, (1st Cir. 2006)(trial court had no authority to order a perjury defendant to pay the costs of investigation and prosecution).

[86] 18 U.S.C. 3663A(b)(1)("The order of restitution shall require that such defendant — (1) in the case of an offense resulting in damage to or loss or destruction of property of a victim of the offense — (A) return the property to the owner of the property or someone designated by the owner; or (B) if return of the property under subparagraph (A) is impossible, impracticable, or inadequate, pay an amount equal to — (i) the greater of — (I) the value of the property on the date of the damage, loss, or destruction; or (II) the value of the property on the date of sentencing, less (ii) the value (as of the date the property is returned) of any part of the property that is returned"). 18 U.S.C. 3663(b)(1)("The order may require that such defendant — (1) in the case of an offense resulting in damage to or loss or destruction of property of a victim of the offense — (A) return the property to the owner of the property or someone designated by the owner; or (B) if return of the property under subparagraph (A) is impossible, impractical, or inadequate, pay an amount equal to the greater of — (i) the value of the property on the date of the damage, loss, or destruction, or (ii) the value of the property on the date of sentencing, less the value (as of the date the property is returned) of any part of the property that is returned").

[87] *United States v. Beydoun*, 469 F.3d 102, 107 (5th Cir. 2006); *United States v. Boccagna*, 450 F.3d 107, 117 (2d Cir. 2006); *United States v. Gordon*, 393 F.3d 1044, 1060 (9th Cir. 2004); *United States v. Dawson*, 250 F.3d 1048, 1050 (7th Cir. 2001).

[88] 18 U.S.C. 3663(c)(1)("Notwithstanding any other provision of law (but subject to the provisions of subsections (a)(1)(B)(i)(II) and (ii), when sentencing a defendant convicted of an offense described in section 401, 408(a), 409, 416, 420, or 422(a) of the Controlled Substances Act (21 U.S.C. 841[drug trafficking], 848(a)[continuing criminal enterprise], 849[drug trafficking at truck stops], 856 [maintaining drug-involved premises], 861 [using children in a drug operation], 863 [trafficking in drug paraphernalia]), in which there is no identifiable victim, the court may order that the defendant make restitution in accordance with this subsection").

[89] 18 U.S.C. 3663(b)(4)("[R]eimburse the victim for lost income and necessary child care, transportation, and other expenses related to participation in the investigation or prosecution of the offense or attendance at proceedings related to the offense"); 18 U.S.C. 3663A(b) (4)(same).

[90] 18 U.S.C. 43(c)("An order of restitution under section 3663 or 3663A of this title with respect to a violation of this section may also include restitution — (1) for the reasonable cost of repeating any experimentation that was interrupted or invalidated as a result of the offense; (2) for the loss of food production or farm income reasonably attributable to the offense; and (3) for any other economic damage, including any losses or costs caused by economic disruption, resulting from the offense").

[91] 18 U.S.C. 228(d)("Upon a conviction under this section, the court shall order restitution under section 3663A in an amount equal to the total unpaid support obligation as it exists at the time of sentencing").

[92] 18 U.S.C. 228(f)(3)("the term 'support obligation' means any amount determined under a court order or an order of an administrative process pursuant to the law of a State or of an Indian tribe to be due from a person for the support and maintenance of a child or of a child and the parent with whom the child is living").

[93] *United States v. Gill*, 264 F.3d 929, 931-33 (9th Cir. 2001).

[94] *United States v. Molak*, 276 F.3d 45, 51 (1st Cir. 2002).

[95] 18 U.S.C. 1593(c)("As used in this section, the term 'victim' means the individual harmed as a result of a crime under this chapter, including, in the case of a victim who is under 18 years of age,

incompetent, incapacitated, or deceased, the legal guardian of the victim or a representative of the victim's estate, or another family member, or any other person appointed as suitable by the court, but in no event shall the defendant be named such representative or guardian").

[96] Chapter 77 of title 18 of the United States Code houses the following criminal prohibitions: 18 U.S.C. 1581 (peonage), 1582 (vessels in the slave trade), 1582 (enticement into slavery), 1584 (sale into involuntary servitude), 1585 (transportation or sale of slaves), 1586 (service on vessels in the slave trade), 1587 (possession of slaves aboard a vessel), 1588 (transportation of slaves from the U.S.), 1589 (forced labor), 1590 (human trafficking), 1591 (sex trafficking), 1592 (documentation in aid of trafficking).

[97] 18 U.S.C. 1593(b)(3)("As used in this subsection, the term 'full amount of the victim's losses' has the same meaning as provided in section 2259(b)(3) and shall in addition include the greater of the gross income or value to the defendant of the victim's services or labor or the value of the victim's labor as guaranteed under the minimum wage and overtime guarantees of the Fair Labor Standards Act (29 U.S.C. 201 et seq.)"). Section 2259(b)(3) (emphasis added) defines "full amount of the victim's losses" to include "any costs incurred by the victim for — (A) medical services relating to physical, psychiatric, or psychological care; (B) physical and occupational therapy or rehabilitation; (C) necessary transportation, temporary housing, and child care expenses; (D) lost income; (E) attorneys' fees, plus any costs incurred in obtaining a civil protection order; and (F) *any other losses suffered by the victim as a proximate result of the offense*."

[98] 18 U.S.C. 2327 (1994 ed.).

[99] "(a) *In general.* — Notwithstanding section 3663 or 3663A, and in addition to any other civil or criminal penalty authorized by law, the court shall order restitution to all victims of any offense for which an enhanced penalty is provided under section 2326. "(b) *Scope and nature of order.* — (1) *Directions.* — The order of restitution under this section shall direct the defendant to pay to the victim (through the appropriate court mechanism) the full amount of the victim's losses as determined by the court pursuant to paragraph (2). (2) *Enforcement.* — An order of restitution under this section shall be issued and enforced in accordance with section 3664 in the same manner as an order under section 3663A. (3) *Definition.* — For purposes of this subsection, the term 'full amount of the victim's losses' means all losses suffered by

the victim as a proximate result of the offense. (4) *Order mandatory.* — (A) The issuance of a restitution order under this section is mandatory. (B) A court may not decline to issue an order under this section because of —(i) the economic circumstances of the defendant; or (ii) the fact that a victim has, or is entitled to, receive compensation for his or her injuries from the proceeds of insurance or any other source. "(c) *Victim defined* — In this section, the term 'victim' has the meaning given that term in section 3663A(a)(2)," 18 U.S.C. 2327.

[100] 18 U.S.C. 3663(c)(2)(A)("An order of restitution under this subsection shall be based on the amount of public harm caused by the offense, as determined by the court in accordance with guidelines promulgated by the United States Sentencing Commission"). Restitution may not be ordered if it appears likely to interfere with a federal forfeiture, 18 U.S.C. 3663(c)(4). The Sentencing Commission has noted the obligation and issued guidelines indicating that community restitution should not take precedence over forfeiture, fines, and special assessments that may otherwise be imposed, U.S.S.G. §5E1.1 Comm. ("*Application Note*: 1. The court shall not order community restitution ... if it appears likely that such an award would interfere with a [federal] forfeiture.... Furthermore, a [federal] penalty assessment ... or a fine ... shall take precedence over an order of community restitution.... *Background*: .. Subsection (d)" replicates 18 U.S.C. 3663(c)(1) and (2)(B) and "implements the instruction to the Commission in section 205 of the Antiterrorism and Effective Death Penalty Act....").

[101] 18 U.S.C. 3663(c)(3)("Restitution under this subsection shall be distributed as follows: (A) 65 percent of the total amount of restitution shall be paid to the State entity designated to administer crime victim assistance in the State in which the crime occurred. (B) 35 percent of the total amount of restitution shall be paid to the State entity designated to receive Federal substance abuse block grant funds").

[102] 18 U.S.C. 3663(c)(2)(B)("In no case shall the amount of restitution ordered under this subsection exceed the amount of the fine which may be ordered for the offense charged in the case").

[103] *United States v. Mansoori*, 304 F.3d 635, 677 (7th Cir. 2002).

[104] 21 U.S.C. 853(q)("The court, when sentencing a defendant convicted of an offense under this subchapter or subchapter II of this chapter involving the manufacture, *the possession, or the possession with intent to distribute,* of amphetamine or methamphetamine, shall —(1) order restitution as provided in sections 3612 and 3664 of Title 18; (2)

order the defendant to reimburse the United States, the State or local government concerned, or both the United States and the State or local government concerned for the costs incurred by the United States or the State or local government concerned, as the case may be, for the cleanup associated with the manufacture of amphetamine or methamphetamine by the defendant *or on premises or in property that the defendant owns, resides, or does business in*; and (3) order restitution to any person injured as a result of the offense as provided in section 3663A of Title 18")(language added by the USA PATRIOT Improvement and Reauthorization Act of 2006 in italics).

[105] *United States v. Gramling*, 417 F.3d 891, 895-96 (8th Cir. 2005)(attempt); *United States v. Lachowski*, 405 F.3d 696, 698-700 (8th Cir. 2005)(possession).

[106] Sec. 743, P.L. 109-177, 120 Stat. 272 (2006).

[107] "[A]n amount equal to the cost of necessary medical and related professional services and devices relating to physical, psychiatric, and psychological care, including nonmedical care and treatment rendered in accordance with a method of healing recognized by the law of the place of treatment," 18 U.S.C. 3663(b)(2)(A), 3663A((b)(2)(A); *e.g., United States v. Ahidley*, 486 F.3d 1184, 1189-190 (10th Cir. 2007).

[108] "[A]n amount equal to the cost of necessary physical and occupational therapy and rehabilitation," 18 U.S.C. 3663(b)(2)(A), 3663A(b)(2)(B).

[109] 18 U.S.C. 3663(b)(2)(C), 3663A(b)(2)(C).

[110] "[L]ost income and necessary child care, transportation, and other expenses incurred during participation in the investigation or prosecution of the offense or attendance at proceedings related to the offense," 18 U.S.C. 3663(b)(4), 3663A(b)(4).

[111] "... [A]n amount equal to the cost of necessary funeral and related services," 18 U.S.C. 3663(b)(3), 3663A(b)(3).

[112] *United States v. Johnson*, 400 F.3d 187, 199-201(4th Cir. 2005)("under the MVRA, a district court properly orders restitution to be paid to a third party when the party bears the cost of providing necessary medical care to a victim of a covered offense who suffered bodily injury as a result of the offense"), quoting, *United States v. Cliatt*, 338 F.3d 1089, 1091 (9th Cir. 2003).

[113] *United States v. Reichow*, 416 F.3d 802, 805-6 (8th Cir. 2005); *United States v. Follet*, 269 F.3d 996, 1001 (9th Cir. 2001); *United States v. Husky*, 924 F.2d 223, 226 (11th Cir. 1991). No such physical injury is required, however, when restitution is order under the authority of individual probation or sexual abuse provisions although sexual abuse

statute may impose greater limits on payments to third parties, *United States v. Follet*, 269 F.3d at 998-1001 (sexual abuse victim); *United States v. Landrum*, 93 F.3d 122, 125-26 (4th Cir. 1996)(probation).

[114] *United States v. Cienfuegos*, 462 F.3d 1160, 1163-169 (9th Cir. 2006); *United States v. Oslund*, 453 F.3d 1048, 1062-63 (8th Cir. 2006)(but explaining that in a given case complications associated with calculating the value of income lost by a murder victim might justify a refusal to award them). Note, however, that while the Ninth Circuit held that restitution for future income can be awarded to the estate or representative of a deceased victim, *United States v. Cienfuegos*, 462 F.3d at 1163-169, it had previously held that the wife of a deceased victim was not entitled to restitution for the victim's lost income *in her own right* unless she also suffered a physical injury as consequence of the offense, *United States v. Dayea*, 73 F.3d 229, 231-32 (9th Cir. 1995).

[115] 18 U.S.C. 3663(b)(4)("[R]eimburse the victim for lost income and necessary child care, transportation, and other expenses related to participation in the investigation or prosecution of the offense or attendance at proceedings related to the offense"); 18 U.S.C. 3663A(b)(4)(same).

[116] *United States v. Malpeso*, 126 F.3d 92, 94-5 (2d Cir. 1997).

[117] *Moore v. United States*, 178 F.3d 994, 1001 (8th Cir. 1999).

[118] *United States v. Cummings*, 281 F.3d 1046, 1052-53 (9th Cir. 2002).

[119] *United States v. Phillips*, 477 F.3d 215, 224 (5th Cir. 2007)(costs incurred by the University of Texas in conducting a computer damage and systems evaluation and contacting individuals whose biographical information and Social Security numbers were stolen from the University's computer system); *United States v. Gordon*, 393 F.3d 1044, 1056-57 (9th Cir. 2004)(cost of company investigation into computer records of an embezzling employee).

[120] *United States v. Phillips*, 367 F.3d 846, 863 (9th Cir. 2004)(in affirming an order to pay restitution to the Environmental Protection Agency for investigation and cleanup costs relating to the offense for which the defendant was convicted, the court noted, "[to] determine whether the Government may receive restitution, we must explore the dividing line between criminal investigation costs (which are not recoverable) and other investigation costs (which are recoverable)").

[121] The crimes in chapters 109A, 110 and 110A of title 18 are found in 18 U.S.C. 2241 (aggravated sexual abuse), 2242 (sexual abuse), 2243 (sexual abuse of a minor or ward), 2244 (abusive sexual contact), 2251

(sexual exploitation of children), 2251A (selling or buying children), 2252 (material involving sexual exploitation of children), 2252A (child pornography), 2252B (misleading Internet domain names), 2252C (misleading Internet words or digital images), 2257 (record keeping requirements), 2257A (simulated sexual conduct records), 2258 (failure to report child abuse), 2260 (overseas production child pornography for the U.S.), 2260A (sex offender registration), 2261 (interstate domestic violence), 2262 (interstate stalking), 2261 (violation of protection orders).

[122] 18 U.S.C. 2248(b)(1), (b)(4)(A); 2259(b)(1), (b)(4)(A); 2264(b)(1), (b)(4)(A).

[123] "For purposes of this section, the term "victim" means the individual harmed as a result of a commission of a crime under this chapter, including, in the case of a victim who is under 18 years of age, incompetent, incapacitated, or deceased, the legal guardian of the victim or representative of the victim's estate, another family member, or any other person appointed as suitable by the court, but in no event shall the defendant be named as such representative or guardian," 18 U.S.C. 2248(c), 2259(c), 2264(c).

[124] "For purposes of this subsection, the term 'full amount of the victim's losses' includes any costs incurred by the victim for — (A) medical services relating to physical, psychiatric, or psychological care; (B) physical and occupational therapy or rehabilitation; (C) necessary transportation, temporary housing, and child care expenses; (D) lost income; (E) attorneys' fees, plus any costs incurred in obtaining a civil protection order; and (F) any other losses suffered by the victim as a proximate result of the offense," 18 U.S.C. 2248(b)(3), 2259(b)(3), 2264(b)(3).

[125] "(B) A court may not decline to issue an order under this section because of — (i) the economic circumstances of the defendant; or (ii) the fact that a victim has, or is entitled to, receive compensation for his or her injuries from the proceeds of insurance or any other source," 18 U.S.C. 2248(b)(4)(B), 2259(b)(4)(B), 2264(b)(4)(B).

[126] "An order of restitution under this section shall be issued and enforced in accordance with section 3664 in the same manner as an order under section 3663A,"18 U.S.C. 2248(b)(2), 2259(b)(2), 2264(b)(2).

[127] "For purposes of this subsection, the term 'full amount of the victim's losses' includes any costs incurred by the victim for ... (F) any other losses suffered by the victim as a proximate result of the offense," 18 U.S.C. 2248(b)(3), 2259(b)(3), 2264(b)(3).

[128] *United States v. Johnson*, 400 F.3d 187, 199-201 (4th Cir. 2005); *United States v. Follet*, 269 F.3d 996, 998-1001 (9th Cir. 2001)(also noting that sections 3663 and 3663A "although broader in these respects than §2248, are narrower in another. Under §3663(b)(2)(A) and §3663A(b)(2)(A), restitution orders can cover psychological care only when there has been a bodily injury, while restitution orders under §2248 are subject to no such limitation").

[129] 18 U.S.C. 3664(a)("For orders of restitution under this title...."); each of the individual provisions also contains a corresponding cross reference, 18 U.S.C. 43(c), 228(d), 1593(b)(2), 2248(b)(2), 2259(b)(2), 2264(b)(2), 2327(b)(2).

[130] 21 U.S.C. 853(q)(1)("The court ... shall — (1) order restitution as provided in sections 3612 and 3663 of Title 18"). Section 3612 provides the procedure for the collection of restitution once it has been ordered.

[131] "For orders of restitution under this title, the court shall order the probation officer to obtain and include in its presentence report, or in a separate report, as the court may direct, information sufficient for the court to exercise its discretion in fashioning a restitution order. The report shall include, to the extent practicable, a complete accounting of the losses to each victim, any restitution owed pursuant to a plea agreement, and information relating to the economic circumstances of each defendant. If the number or identity of victims cannot be reasonably ascertained, or other circumstances exist that make this requirement clearly impracticable, the probation officer shall so inform the court," 18 U.S.C. 3664(a); *United States v. Milkiewicz*, 470 F.3d 390, 403 (1st Cir. 2006); *United States v. Murry*, 395 F.3d 712, 720 (7th Cir. 2005); *United States v. Gordon*, 393 F.3d 1044, 1056 (9th Cir. 2004).

[132] 18 U.S.C. 3664(d)(1)("Upon the request of the probation officer, but not later than 60 days prior to the date initially set for sentencing, the attorney for the Government, after consulting, to the extent practicable, with all identified victims, shall promptly provide the probation officer with a listing of the amounts subject to restitution").

[133] 18 U.S.C. 3664(d)(2)("The probation officer shall, prior to submitting the presentence report under subsection (a), to the extent practicable — (A) provide notice to all identified victims of — (i) the offense or offenses of which the defendant was convicted; (ii) the amounts subject to restitution submitted to the probation officer; (iii) the opportunity of the victim to submit information to the probation

officer concerning the amount of the victim's losses; (iv) the scheduled date, time, and place of the sentencing hearing; (v) the availability of a lien in favor of the victim pursuant to subsection (m)(1)(B); and (vi) the opportunity of the victim to file with the probation officer a separate affidavit relating to the amount of the victim's losses subject to restitution; and (B) provide the victim with an affidavit form to submit pursuant to subparagraph (A)(vi)").

[134] 18 U.S.C. 3664(d)(3)("Each defendant shall prepare and file with the probation officer an affidavit fully describing the financial resources of the defendant, including a complete listing of all assets owned or controlled by the defendant as of the date on which the defendant was arrested, the financial needs and earning ability of the defendant and the defendant's dependents, and such other information that the court requires relating to such other factors as the court deems appropriate").

[135] 18 U.S.C. 3664(e); *United States v. Bryson*, 485 F.3d 1205, (D.C. Cir. 2007); *United States v. Danford*, 435 F.3d 682, 689 (7th Cir. 2006); *United States v. Tarbox*, 361 F.3d 664, 666 (1st Cir. 2004); *United States v. Smith*, 344 F.3d 479, 484 (6th Cir. 2003); *United States v. Young*, 272 F.3d 1052, 1056 (8th Cir. 2001).

[136] 18 U.S.C. 3664(e); *United States v. Pierce*, 479 F.3d 546 (8th Cir. 2007); *United States v. Beydoun*, 469 F.3d 102, 197 (5th Cir. 2006); *United States v. Prochner*, 416 F.3d 54, 65 (1st Cir. 2005); *United States v. Wilson*, 416 F.3d 1164, 1170 (10th Cir. 2005); *United States v. Murry*, 395 F.3d 712, 721 (7th Cir. 2005). In addition at least one circuit has held that "section 3664(d) authorizes the district court to allow a victim to prove up his own claim for restitution," *United States v. Gamma Tech Industries, Inc.*, 265 F.3d 917, 924-25 (9th Cir. 2001).

[137] 18 U.S.C. 3664(e); *United States v. Wood*, 364 F.3d 704, 714-15 (6th Cir. 2004); *United States v. Wilson*, 416 F.3d 1164, 1170 (10th Cir. 2005); *United States v. Tarbox*, 361 F.3d 664, 666 (1st Cir. 2004).

[138] 18 U.S.C. 3664(f)(1)(A); *United States v. Senty-Haugen*, 449 F.3d 862, 865 (8th Cir. 2006); *United States v. Sosebee*, 419 F.3d 451, 460 (6th Cir. 2005); *United States v. Reifler*, 446 F.3d 65, 133 (2d Cir. 2006)(internal citations omitted) ("[T]he government, though arguing that the actual ... figures as to shareholder losses were $10-13 million, believed the court could properly cap it at the $6.092 million figure. Such a cap for restitution purposes, however, plainly contravenes the MVRA's requirement that any restitution order compensate the victims in 'full'"). Nevertheless, victims are not entitled to more than full compensation; restitution may not be ordered for amounts in

excess of the victim losses, *United States v. Boccagna*, 450 F.3d 107, (2d Cir. 2006); *United States v. Leahy*, 438 F.3d 328, 337 (3d Cir. 2006); *United States v. Gordon*, 383 F.3d 1044, 1060 (9th Cir. 2004); *United States v. Dawson*, 250 F.3d 1048, 1050 (7th Cir. 2001).

[139] 18 U.S.C. 3664(f)(2).

[140] 18 U.S.C. 3664(f)(3)(A); *United States v. Jaffe*, 417 F.3d 259, 265 (2d Cir. 2005); *United States v. Wilson*, 416 F.3d 1164, 1170 (10th Cir. 2005); *United States v. Sensmeier*, 361 F.3d 982, 990 (7th Cir. 2004).

[141] 18 U.S.C. 3664(f)(4); *United States v. Simmonds*, 235 F.3d 826, 832 (3d Cir. 2000)(since restitution may take the form of replacement, a district court may validly consider replacement costs in assessing a victim's losses); *but see*, *United States v. Fazal-Ur-Raheman-Fazal*, 355 F.3d 40, (1st Cir. 2004)(a defendant guilty of international parental kidnaping cannot be ordered to make restitution in the form of a return or transfer of the kidnapped children to their mother either as property or as a service under section 3663(f)(4): "Children are not 'property' nor is their transfer a 'service,' and we decline the invitation to hold otherwise").

[142] 18 U.S.C. 3664(f)(3)(B); *United States v. Day*, 418 F.3d 746, 758 (7th Cir. 2005).

[143] *United States v. Ahidley*, 486 F.3d 1184, 1191-193 (10th Cir. 2007); *United States v. Thigpen*, 456 F.3d 766, 771 (7th Cir. 2006)("[W]e explicitly oppose[ ] a district court's attempt to minimize its responsibility to set a restitution schedule by ordering 'immediate' payment. Such an arrangement effectively transfers the district court's responsibility for setting a restitution schedule to the probation office, which is inconsistent with the statute"); *United States v. Gunning*, 401 F.3d 1145, 1149-150 (9th Cir. 2005).

[144] 18 U.S.C. 3664(f)(1)(B); *United States v. Cienfuegos*, 462 F.3d 1160, (9th Cir. 2006) (civil litigation); *United States v. Ruff*, 420 F.3d 772, 774 (8th Cir. 2005)(forfeiture); *United States v. Doe*, 374 F.3d 851, 856 (9th Cir. 2004); *but see*, *United States v. McCracken*, 487 F.3d 1125, 1128-129 (8th Cir. 2007)(court held that the amount of restitution ordered might include money the government seized from the defendant bank robber when he was arrested and had yet to turn over to the bank or the court, but assumed that when it did so the amount of restitution owed would be reduced accordingly). Of course, the plea agreement may stipulate the restitution owed the government may be offset by the proceeds of a forfeiture, *see e.g.*, *United States v. Miller*, 406 F.3d 323, 327-28 (5th Cir. 2005).

[145] 18 U.S.C. 3664(d)(5).

[146] 18 U.S.C. 3664(d)(5).

[147] 18 U.S.C. 3664(d)(5).

[148] *United States v. Kapelushnik*, 306 F.3d 1090, 1093-94 (11th Cir. 2002); *United States v. Jolivette*, 257 F.3d 581, 584 (6th Cir. 2001).

[149] *United States v. Terlingo*, 327 F.3d 216, 219 (3d Cir. 2003); *United States v. Reano*, 298 F.3d 1208, 1212-213 (10th Cir. 2002); *United States v. Stevens*, 211 F.3d 1, 5 (2d Cir. 2000).

[150] *United States v. Cienfuegos*, 462 F.3d 1160, 1162-163 (9th Cir. 2006)("However, because Cienfuegos fails to demonstrate actual prejudice from the government's failure to comply with the procedural requirements of section 3664, the only entity to suffer prejudice here was Noline's estate. Therefore, we hold that any error the district court may have made in considering the government's untimely future lost income motion was harmless"); *United States v. Johnson*, 400 F.3d 187, (4th Cir. 2005)("Thus, just as the failure to conform with the ninety-day limit constitutes harmless error absent prejudice, so too does the failure to comply with the ten-day limit. Johnson has failed to show any prejudice from the postponement of his restitution hearing. He had notice of the amount sought, and the court held a lengthy hearing before entering the restitution order"); *United States v. Chael*, 389 F.3d 35, 48-50 (1st Cir. 2004); *United States v. Zakhary*, 357 F.3d 186, 191 (2d Cir. 2004).

[151] *United States v. Pawlinski*, 374 F.3d 436, 539-41 (7th Cir. 2004)(except pursuant to a plea bargain or on assignment by a victim, the court has no authority to award restitution to the Crime Victims Fund); *United States v. Johnson*, 378 F.3d 230, 245 (2d Cir. 2004)("Hunter also urges us to vacate the District Court's restitution award on the basis that it was error for the District Court to assign Felix's interest in restitution, should Felix renounce it, to the Crime Victims Fund. Hunter argues that §3664(g)(2) provides the statutory authority to assign interest in restitution only to victims, and that the Court therefore had no authority to do so. We disagree").

[152] 18 U.S.C. 3664(h). A sentencing court may apportion restitution, *United States v. Ingles*, 445 F.3d 830, 838-39 (5th Cir. 2006), but it has no authority to order that restitution not be joint and severable, *United States v. Klein*, 476 F.3d 111, 114 (2d Cir. 2007)(trial court erroneously believed the Probation Service incapable of administering joint and severable restitution awards).

[153] *United States v. Scott*, 270 F.3d 30, 52 (1st Cir. 2001)("If the defendants are each made liable for the full amount, but the victim may recover no more than the total loss, the implication is that each defendant's liability ends when the victim is made whole, regardless of the actual contributions of individual defendants"); *United States v. Nucci*, 364 F.3d 419, 423 (2d Cir. 2004); *United States v. Adeniji*, 221 F.3d 1020, 1029 (7th Cir. 1999). Other courts reach the same result — victims are not entitled to the enforcement of joint and several restitution orders beyond the point of full recovery — by reading together sections 3664(f)(1) (A)(full amount of victim's losses) and 3664(j)(2)(restitution offset by subsequent victim recovery in civil litigation), *United States v. Dawson*, 250 F.3d 1048, 1050 (7th Cir. 2001); *United States v. Stanley*, 309 F.3d 611, 613 (9th Cir. 2002).

[154] 18 U.S.C. 3664(i)("... In any case in which the United States is a victim, the court shall ensure that all other victims receive full restitution before the United States receives any restitution").

[155] *United States v. Senty-Haugen*, 449 F.3d 862, 865 (8th Cir. 2006); *United States v. Ekanem*, 383 F.3d 40, 43 (2d Cir. 2004).

[156] *United States v. Alalade*, 204 F.3d 536, 539-41 (4th Cir. 2000); *United States v. Doe*, 374 F.3d 851, 856 (9th Cir. 2004); *United States v. Ruff*, 472 F.3d 1044, 1047 (8th Cir. 2007)

[157] 18 U.S.C. 3664(j)(1).

[158] 18 U.S.C. 3664(j)(2). The courts, however, tend to read the section broadly as part of general intent to compensate victims fully but not to award them a windfall, *see e.g.*, *United States v. McDaniel*, 398 F.3d 540, (6th Cir. 2005)("the restitution statutes do not permit victims to obtain multiple recoveries for the same loss. *See* 18 U.S.C. 35664(j)(2)"). Yet, the defendant bears the burden of establishing that the civil recovery corresponds to the injury for which restitution was ordered, *United States v. Calbat*, 266 F.3d 358, 365 (5th Cir. 2001).

[159] 18 U.S.C. 3664(k)("A restitution order shall provide that the defendant shall notify the court and the Attorney General of any material change in the defendant's economic circumstances that might affect the defendant's ability to pay restitution. The court may also accept notification of a material change in the defendant's economic circumstances from the United States or from the victim. The Attorney General shall certify to the court that the victim or victims owed restitution by the defendant have been notified of the change in circumstances. Upon receipt of the notification, the court may, on its own motion, or the motion of any party, including the victim, adjust

the payment schedule, or require immediate payment in full, as the interests of justice require"). Section 3664 deals specifically with one charge in the defendant's financial circumstances by requiring that he apply any windfall he receives while in prison to his obligation to make restitution, 18 U.S.C. 3664(n)("If a person obligated to provide restitution, or pay a fine, receives substantial resources from any source, including inheritance, settlement, or other judgment, during a period of incarceration, such person shall be required to apply the value of such resources to any restitution or fine still owed").

[160] *United States v. Vanhorn*, 399 F.3d 884, 886 (8th Cir. 2005)(defendant's desire to begin saving while in prison for the future costs of medical treatment provided at government expense pending his release does not constitute a change in economic circumstances for purposes of section 3664(k)).

[161] *United States v. Grant*, 235 F.3d 95, 100 (2d Cir. 2000)("it cannot be that a court's later understanding that it had sentenced a defendant without full knowledge of his assets alone constitutes a material change in economic circumstances. A change of the sort contemplated by the statute is identified by an objective comparison of a defendant's financial condition before and after a sentence is imposed").

[162] 18 U.S.C. 3583(e)(3), 3565(a).

[163] 18 U.S.C. 3613(c).

[164] *United States v. Novak*, 476 F.3d 1041, 1044 (9th Cir. 2007)(For enforcement of restitution orders, 18 U.S.C. 3664(m)(1)(A)(i) and 3613(f) authorize recourse to the fine collection authority of section 3613. For collection of unpaid fines, 18 U.S.C. 3613(a) authorizes the use of the practices and procedures available for enforcement of a civil judgment. The Federal Debt Collection Procedure Act is available for such purposes, 28 U.S.C. 3001).

[165] 18 U.S.C. 3664(m)(1)(B)("At the request of a victim named in a restitution order, the clerk of the court shall issue an abstract of judgment certifying that a judgment has been entered in favor of such victim in the amount specified in the restitution order. Upon registering, recording, docketing, or indexing such abstract in accordance with the rules and requirements relating to judgments of the court of the State where the district court is located, the abstract of judgment shall be a lien on the property of the defendant located in such State in the same manner and to the same extent and under the same conditions as a judgment of a court of general jurisdiction in that State").

[166] 18 U.S.C. 3771(a)(6), (d)(3). Mandamus is an extraordinary form of judicial review which is only rarely granted. In the case of section 3771, however, since Congress had designated mandamus as the principal avenue of review, the courts have not required victims to overcome the hurdles typically faced by a petitioner seeking review of a district court determination through a writ of mandamus but instead have held the enforcement of section 3771 by lower courts to an abuse of discretion standard of mandamus review, *In re W.R.Huff Asset Management Co., LLC,* 409 F.3d 555, 562-63 (2d Cir. 2005); *Kenna v. United States District Court*, 435 F.3d 1011, 1017 (9th. Cir. 2006).

[167] 18 U.S.C. 3664(*l*).

[168] *Durham v. United States*, 401 U.S. 481, 48-82 (1971)("The status of abatement caused by death on direct review has recently been discussed by the Court of Appeals for the Eighth Circuit in *Crooker v. United States*, 325 F.2d 318. In reviewing the case that court concluded that the lower federal courts are unanimous on the rule to the be applied: death pending direct review of a criminal conviction abates not only the appeal but also all proceedings had in the prosecution from its inception.... We believe they have adopted the correct rule"). The Supreme Court later cryptically called the vitality of *Durham* into question when it announced that, "The Court is advised that the petitioner died at New Bern, N.C., on November 14, 1975. The petition for certiorari is therefore dismissed. To the extent that *Durham v. United States*, 401 U.S. 481 (1971), may be inconsistent with this ruling, *Durham* is overruled," *Dove v. United States*, 423 U.S. 325, 325 (1976). The lower federal courts apparently understand *Dove* to mean that death during the pendency of a certiorari petition does not abate the underlying proceedings, but that otherwise the statement from *Durham* remains in effect, see *United States v. Pogue*, 19 F.3d 663, 665 (D.C.Cir. 1994), quoting the statement from *Durham* and citing post-*Dove* findings in accord from the Second, Fourth, Fifth, Seventh, Eighth, Tenth and Eleventh Circuits.

[169] *United States v. Estate of Parsons*, 367 F.3d 409 (5th Cir. 2004)(en banc)("regardless of its purpose, the order of restitution cannot stand in the wake of Parsons's death. Because he now is deemed never to have been convicted or even charged, the order of restitution abates *ab initio*"); *United States v. Logal*, 106 F.3d 1547, 1152 (11th Cir. 1997)("Under the doctrine of abatement ab initio, however, the defendant stands as if he never had been convicted. The absence of a

conviction precludes imposition of the restitution order against Kuczek or his estate pursuant to §3663"); *United States v. Wright*, 160 F.3d 905, 909 (2d Cir. 1998) (Leslie having died prior to the completion of his prison term, however, his restitutionary payments will never come due ... the time for him to commence making payments can never arrive, the retention of the restitution order would be an act of futility. We therefore conclude that the order of restitution should be abated. We leave for another day such questions as whether an order that makes restitution payable immediately should generally survive the death of the defendant during the pendency of his direct appeal as of right...."); *United States v. Lay*, 456 F.Supp.2d 869, 875 (S.D.Tex. 2006); *contra*, *United States v. Christopher*, 273 F.3d 294, 299 (3d Cir. 2001) ("We are persuaded that abatement should not apply to the order of restitution in this case, thus, it survives against the estate of the deceased convict"); *United States v. Dudley*, 739 F.2d 175, 178 (4th Cir. 1984).

In: Fines and Restitutions... ISBN: 978-1-60456-589-8
Editor: P. N. Allerton Jr., pp. 51-60

Chapter 2

CRIMINAL RESTITUTION IN THE 110TH CONGRESS: A SKETCH*

Charles Doyle
American Law Division

ABSTRACT

Restitution legislation in the 110th Congress falls into three categories. Some proposals, such as the gang crime bills, create new federal crimes or amend specific existing federal offenses and in doing so include specific restitution provisions particular to those offenses, e.g., H.R. 880, H.R. 1582, H.R. 1692, S. 456, and S. 990 (gang bills); and H.R. 871 (spousal support). Other proposals address a particular aspect of the law such as abatement which limits restitution collection after the defendant's death (S. 149). Two bills — H.R. 845, the Criminal Restitution Improvement Act, and S. 973, the Restitution for Victims of Crime Act — make substantial changes in federal restitution law. The proposals call for three kinds of adjustments: (1) an expansion of offenses for which restitution may be ordered without recourse to the laws relating to probation and supervised release; (2) an overhaul of the procedures governing the issuance and enforcement of restitution orders to afford prosecutors greater enforcement flexibility without having to seek the approval of the sentencing court; and (3) authority for preindictment and presentencing restraining orders and other

* Excerpted from CRS Report RS22709, dated August 22, 2007.

protective measures to prevent dissipation of assets by those who may subsequently owe restitution. Although similar in many respects, S. 973 more closely resembles the proposals transmitted by the Justice Department. The provisions of H.R. 845 also appear as Title V of the Violent Crime Control Act of 2007 (H.R. 3156/S. 1860).

This is an abridged version of CRS Report RL34139, *Criminal Restitution Proposals in the 110th Congress*. Related reports include CRS Report RL34138, Restitution in Federal Criminal Cases, and CRS Report RS22708, Restitution in Federal Criminal Cases: A Sketch, by Charles Doyle.

INTRODUCTION

Restitution is the act of restoring an individual or entity in whole or in part to the lost circumstances they might have once enjoyed. In a federal criminal context, it is the order of a sentencing court directing a defendant to reimburse or otherwise compensate the victims of his crimes. Restitution is based on the losses suffered by the victims of a crime. Neither the defendant's financial condition at the time of sentencing, nor his future economic prospects figure in the amount of restitution awarded.

Consequently, in some cases the amount of restitution ordered may exceed what the defendant can ever reasonably be expected to pay, particularly in the case of mandatory restitution. Nevertheless, there have been suggestions that in other instances insufficient restitution has been ordered or collected because of the particularities of restitution law.

RESTITUTION FOR NEW CRIMES

Existing federal law outlaws the commission of various federal crimes by street gangs. There have been a number of proposals to amend or augment the existing federal offense. They include H.R. 880 (Representative Forbes), H.R. 1582 (Representative Schiff), H.R. 1692 (Representative Pallone), S. 456 (Senator Feinstein), S. 990 (Senator Menendez). In each instance the proposal permits the courts to order restitution as part of the sentence imposed for violation of their newly created or newly amended offenses. Existing federal law outlaws certain failures to pay child support and requires the court to award restitution upon conviction. H.R. 871

(Representative Wexler) proposes to outlaw the failure to pay court-ordered spousal property distribution and requires the court to award restitution upon conviction.

ABATEMENT

Upon the death of a defendant pending appeal the courts treat his indictment and conviction as if they had never occurred. The case is returned to the lower federal court with instructions to vacate the conviction and to dismiss the indictment. The circuit courts are somewhat more divided on the question of whether a restitution order likewise abates upon the death of the defendant pending appeal. In the twilight of the 109th Congress, the Senate passed legislation that would have barred abatement of a restitution order. The bill's sponsor, Senator Feinstein, reintroduced essentially the same proposal as S. 149 in the 110th Congress.

H.R. 845 (MANDATORY RESTITUTION)

H.R. 845 introduced by Representative Chabot replaces the discretionary and mandatory restitution provisions of sections 3663 and 3663A with a revised Section 3663. Existing law requires restitution for crimes of violence, maintaining a drug-involved premises, and when prohibited in Title18, fraud and crimes against property. It permits a court to order restitution for crimes otherwise proscribed in Title18, as well as for various aviation safety and drug offenses, and as a condition for probation and supervised release. It does not call for restitution in the case of most securities offenses, environmental offenses, drug offenses, or most of the other property crimes outlawed in other titles of the Code. H.R. 845 requires restitution for all federal offenses that result in qualified losses to qualified victims.

Existing law defines "victims" for purposes of mandatory restitution as (1) those designated victims in a plea agreement, (2) the estate of deceased victims, (3) those directly and proximately harmed by a qualifying offense, (4) those harmed by the scheme, conspiracy, or pattern of criminal activity of a defendant convicted of a qualifying offense which has as one its elements such a scheme, conspiracy, or pattern of criminal activity, and (5) in the case of children, the incompetent, incapacitated, or deceased, legal guardians, family members, and other representatives. H.R. 845 describes five classes of victims who are entitled to mandatory restitution: (1) Identifiable individuals and entities who suffer a pecuniary loss proximately caused by the offense; (2) Identifiable individuals and entities who suffer a pecuniary loss as a consequence of a physical injury to another proximately caused by the offense; (3) The successors to any such direct or third-party victims; (4) Anyone the parties agree to in a plea bargain; and (5) Anyone otherwise provided by law, id.

Existing law portrays the restitution to be awarded in the case of qualifying offenses involving the loss or destruction of property in one way (return and/or payment of the lost value) and that to be awarded in the case of qualifying offenses involving physical injuries in another (medical expenses, costs of rehabilitation, funeral costs when the victim has been killed, and the victims' expenses relating to their participation in the investigation and prosecution of the qualifying offense). H.R. 845 treats the losses covered by restitution in much the same way it treats the definition of victim and inventory of qualifying offenses. It adopts some features of existing law, and it changes others. It carries forward the language under which restitution orders must include "in the case of an offense resulting in the death of the victim, an amount equal to the cost of necessary funeral and related services." It uses the same language to describe restitution for lost income, medical expenses, and the cost of rehabilitation — with a difference. Existing law makes them a matter of mandatory restitution only with respect to offenses involving physical injuries. H.R. 845 calls for restitution regardless of the nature of the crime. Its vindication expenses clause runs parallel to existing law, but makes specific allowance to cover the costs of attorneys other than those employed by the government.

S. 973 (Discretionary Restitution)

S. 973's expansion of authority to order restitution is far more selective than that of H.R. 845. It amends Section 3663 to permit a federal court to order restitution following conviction for certain (1) Federal Water Pollution Control Act offenses; (2) Marine Protection, Research, and Sanctuaries Act offenses; (3) Act to Prevent Pollution from Ships offenses; (4) Safe Drinking Water Act offenses; (5) Solid Waste Disposal Act offenses; and (6) Clean Air Act offenses. S. 973 amends the discretionary and mandatory restitution provisions of sections 3663 and 3663A to permit victims to recover related attorney fees other than those of government attorneys.

PROCEDURAL ADJUSTMENTS (H.R. 845)

The procedure for issuing a restitution order is laid out in 18 U.S.C. 3664. Following conviction, a probation officer conducts an investigation, collects information from the prosecutor, victims and defendant, and prepares a report for the court which is shared with the parties. The court conducts a hearing to resolve any questions relating to whether a particular individual is a victim entitled to restitution, whether a particular loss is one that qualifies for restitution, and the specifics of the defendant's ability to pay. Court-issued restitution orders may direct the defendant to pay in a lump sum, in installments, in-kind or in some combination of the three. Until full restitution is made, the court may modify its order to reflect any change in the defendant's financial circumstances. The Justice Department contends that the role which the statute assigns to the courts impedes effective collection of restitution and has recommended amendments.

H.R. 845's amendments are intended to permit the court to establish a payment schedule, but to allow the government to formulate one if the court does not. Moreover, the fact that the court has established a payment schedule does not prevent the government from supplementing the effort with other collection measures taken without the need to seek the sentencing court's approval. H.R. 845 drops the statement now found in Section 3664(c) that identifies the external provisions of law that govern the proceedings. Among the provisions now said to govern the proceedings is Rule 32(c)(2) of the Federal Rules of Criminal Procedure, which states that, "the probation officer who interviews a defendant as part of a presentence investigation must, on request, give the defendant's attorney notice and a reasonable opportunity to attend the interview."

Whether H.R. 845 intends or accomplishes a repeal of the Rule for purposes of restitution interviews is unclear. Defendants continue to have the opportunity and obligation to notify the court and the government of any change in their financial situation. H.R. 845 adds a further requirement that victims notify the court if they change their name or mailing address. It also amends existing law to prolong a defendant's probationary period and term of supervised release as long as restitution is still owed, although during the extension the obligation to pay restitution is the only condition that remains in effect.

PROCEDURAL ADJUSTMENTS (S. 973)

Like H.R. 845, more than a few of S. 973's amendments have been crafted to provide alternatives to direct involvement of the sentencing court in restitution enforcement. The approach of S. 973 to judicial scheduling of installment payments is much like of H.R. 845. The Bureau of Prisons has a program designed to ensure that federal inmates meet their financial responsibilities which requires them to have a financial plan to meet those obligations from the money they earn from prison work assignments if nothing else. The Justice Department's *Analysis* claims that appellate decisions requiring sentencing courts to maintain control over installment payment plans effectively prohibits the BOP from enforcing final restitution orders through its long established program.

Under existing law, a prosecutor's options when enforcing a restitution order include the inmate financial responsibility program, liens against the defendant's property, and garnishment of the defendant's wages or amounts in his pension plan. A court, however, may stay execution of a restitution order pending appeal. S. 973 dictates that any stay pending appeal that curtails a prosecutor's ability to enforce a restitution order in the interim must be for good cause stated on the record. It also seems to narrow the court's discretion over the protective orders that may accompany a stay. In addition, S. 973 states that the issuance of such mandatory protective measures should not be construed as a limitation on the authority of prosecutors to continue their restitution-related investigations and enforcement efforts.

Under the Federal Rules of Criminal Procedure, the probation officer's sentencing report may not include certain medical, confidential or informant-related material. The Rules also forbid disclosing matters occurring before a federal grand jury, subject to certain exceptions, some of which require court approval and some of which do not. Various other statutes prohibit the disclosure of financial information but recognize an exception for information provided under grand jury subpoena. Those statutes may be thought to proscribe disclosure beyond the grand jury absent some additional grant of authority. There are no statutory provisions which specifically proscribe Bureau of Prisons officials from disclosing to prosecutors information relating to an inmate's ability to pay restitution. S. 973 grants the United States Attorneys access without court approval to financial information on the defendant held by a grand jury, the Probation Office, or the Bureau of Prisons in order to enforce restitution orders. The Justice Department has explained that the change is necessary because some district courts insist upon court approval before allowing prosecutors to examine probation officer reports on a defendant's financial condition. They do not explain why explicit authority for access to grand jury material and Bureau of Prison records is necessary or why court approval constitutes an obstacle.

S. 973 has several provisions designed to prevent the dissipation of assets following the issuance of the original restitution order. For instance, every restitution order must include an instruction that the defendant is to refrain from any action that would conceal or dissipate his assets. The court ordering restitution may direct the defendant to bring crime-related property within the jurisdiction of the court. It may at any time enter a protective order to ensure the availability of assets for restitution purposes. And it may craft or modify a restitution order to reflect the fact that the defendant has concealed or dissipated assets.

H.R. 845/S. 973: SECTION 3664A (ASSET PRESERVATION)

H.R. 845 and S. 973 add virtually identical asset preservation components to the restitution procedure in the form of a new 18 U.S.C. 3664A. The asset preservation features of Section 3664A contemplate judicial asset freeze orders and other protective measures before conviction, both before and after indictment. The procedure draws upon, and in part is modeled after, the protective order features of the criminal forfeiture section of the Controlled Substances Act. In some ways, the model may seem like a less than perfect fit. The title to forfeitable property vests in the United States when the confiscation-triggering offense is committed. Restitution has no comparable feature. At the time of the passage of the Controlled Substance Act, property used to facilitate the commission of a forfeiture-triggering offense could be confiscated in a civil proceeding upon a showing of probable cause. Restitution requires conviction of the property owner; civil forfeiture does not.

On the other hand, proponents might well point out that some of the differences between forfeiture and restitution argue for greater protective tools in the case of restitution. The government is the beneficiary of confiscation; the victims of crime are the beneficiaries of restitution. A victim is likely to feel the loss of restitution more sharply than the government the loss of forfeitable property. As for the availability of a civil forfeiture equivalent, proponents might note that under existing law, authorities may use a search warrant to seize the fruits of crime based on the probable cause. The protective orders envisioned in H.R. 845 and S. 973 either involve property traceable to a particular offense or can only be issued in the interest of justice. They are not administrative commands, but are court-issued protective measures, and come with the prospect of a judicial hearing to contest their issuance.

The task of assessing the relative strengths and weaknesses of proposed Section 3664A is made more complicated by its occasional want of clarity. Notwithstanding the Justice Department's guidance, the text is sometimes perplexing. It seems fairly certain that the bills mean to establish the following procedure in the case of post-indictment orders. Courts would be authorized to issue an ex parte protective order upon a probable cause showing that (1) the defendant had been indicted for an offense for which restitution might be ordered, (2) that the offense or offenses had resulted in qualified losses to qualified victims of an approximate amount for which the defendant would be obligated to make restitution if convicted of the offense or offenses charged, (3) the value of the property to be restrained or the amount of the bond to be posted did not greatly exceed the approximate amount of restitution that might be awarded, and (4) (perhaps) the property is traceable to the offense charged.

A defendant would be entitled to a hearing upon a prima facie showing that the value of property restrained or the amount of the bond greatly exceeded the amount of the restitution that could be ordered; or that the law does not authorize restitution for the offense, victim, or losses claimed in the order; or (if court relies on the traceable property prong of proposed Section 3664A(a)(1)(A)) that the property restrained is not traceable to the offense charged. Even then, a hearing could be granted only if the defendant could also show by a preponderance of the evidence that the order had or would deprive him of defense counsel of his choice or deprive him or his family of the necessities of life. If the defendant is able to meet this burden — or whatever reduced burden due process demands — he is entitled to a hearing at which the government may contest his challenge. After which, the court may modify its protective order should it find either (1) a want of probable cause to believe that the restrained property or at least all of it would be needed to satisfy any restitution order under the facts of the case or (2) (if the "traceable property" authority was relied upon) a want of probable cause to believe that the restrained property, or some of it, is traceable to the offense charged, or (3)(perhaps or at least to the extent due process requires) that a failure to modify the order would deny the defendant defense counsel of his choice or would impose an undue hardship upon the defendant or his family.

It seems likely that is what S. 973 and H.R. 845 intend; it is not literally what they state.

As for preindictment protective orders, the bills declare that applications and orders are to be governed by 21 U.S.C. 853(e) and proposed Section 3664A. This should probably be understood to say that proposed Section 3664A governs in cases of conflict with Section 853(e). Prior to indictment, Section 853(e) requires that the property owner be given notice and an opportunity for a hearing, unless the government establishes by probable cause that the property will become unavailable if prior notice is given. The bills seem to make the initial issuance of the restraining order ex parte in all cases. Such ex parte restraining orders are temporary, good for only ten days unless extended for cause. Absent an indictment, the restraining order is only good for ninety days, again unless extended for cause. Section 3664A does not describe the post-restraint hearing to be held in preindictment cases. Section 853(e)(1)(B) indicates that upon application of the United States, the court may enter protective orders to preserve the availability of property which the government asserts is subject to criminal forfeiture prior to indictment if it finds the government is likely to prevail on the issue and the government's need for availability outweighs any hardship of the property owner. Third parties may move for modification of a restraining order on the grounds of hardship and less onerous alternatives. At least on the face of things, third parties may not move to have a restraining order modified on the grounds that the property restrained belongs to them rather than to the defendant, although they may do so at the conclusion of the criminal case.

H.R. 845/S 973 (Anti-Crime Injunction Expansion)

Traditionally, the federal courts will not enjoin the commission of a crime unless expressly authorized to do so by statute. As part of the Comprehensive Crime Control Act of 1984, Congress enacted 18 U.S.C. 1345 which authorized the federal courts to enjoin the commission of various fraud offenses and to freeze property derived from some of these offenses, namely, banking law or health care offenses. H.R. 845 and S. 973 each enlarge Section 1345 to authorize both injunctions and freeze orders relating to any federal offenses for which restitution might be ordered. Their reach is somewhat different since their view of offenses for which restitution may be ordered is different. For H.R. 845, it is any federal offense which proximately causes another pecuniary loss. For S. 973, it is the mandatory restitution crimes, that is, any federal crime of violence, property damage, fraud, and product tampering, as well as the discretionary restitution crimes, that is, any other crime proscribed in Title18, the various aircraft safety and drug offenses, and the environmental crimes that S. 973 adds to the restitution list. Given the wide-ranging freeze orders that the bills make available elsewhere, the freeze order component of their amendment of Section 1345 may be considered unnecessary.

In: Fines and Restitutions... ISBN: 978-1-60456-589-8
Editor: P. N. Allerton Jr., pp. 61-68

Chapter 3

RESTITUTION IN FEDERAL CRIMINAL CASES: A SKETCH*

Charles Doyle
American Law Division

ABSTRACT

Federal courts may not order a defendant to pay restitution to the victims of his or her crimes unless authorized to do so. Several statutes supply such authorization. For instance, federal courts are statutorily required to order victim restitution when sentencing a defendant for a felony that constitutes either a crime of violence or an offense against property, including fraud or deceit proscribed in title 18 of the United States Code. The obligation exists even if the defendant is indigent, and restitution must take the form of in-kind or installment payments. Moreover, a court may not order restitution as required by the statute and then grant the defendant remission of restitution. Ordinarily, however, restitution is available only to victims who have suffered a physical injury or financial loss as a direct and proximate consequence of the crime of conviction, and only to the extent of their losses. In addition, federal courts are permitted to order victim restitution when sentencing a defendant for various controlled substance and aviation safety offenses, or any felony proscribed in Title 18 of the *United States Code* for which

---

* Excerpted from CRS Report RS22708, dated August 22, 2007.

restitution is not mandatory. Moreover, a federal court may make restitution a condition of probation or supervised release.

When restitution is to be ordered, a probation officer prepares a report after gathering information from victims, the government, and the defendant. The parties receive copies of the report and may contest its recommendations. The court has considerable discretion as to the manner and scheduling of restitution payments, but the authority may not be delegated to probation or prison officials. Furthermore, the order must provide for full restitution for all victims unless the sheer number of victims or the complications of a given case preclude such an order.

This is an abridged version of a longer report, CRS Report RL34138, *Restitution in Federal Criminal Cases*, without the footnotes and citations to authority found in the longer report. Related reports include CRS Report RL34139, *Criminal Restitution Proposals in the 110th Congress*, available in an abridged version as CRS Report RS22709, *Criminal Restitution in the 110th Congress: A Sketch*, all by Charles Doyle.

BACKGROUND

The Victim and Witness Protection Act of 1982 (VWPA) vested federal courts with discretion to order restitution in any criminal case arising out of Title 18 of the *United States Code* or in air piracy cases. The Violent Crime Control and Law Enforcement Act of 1994 established mandatory restitution as a feature of the federal criminal prohibitions on sexual abuse, sexual exploitation of children, and domestic violence. The Mandatory Victim Restitution Act (MVRA) portion of the Antiterrorism and Effective Death Penalty Act of 1996 made mandatory restitution a consequence of conviction in most serious federal criminal cases (i.e., crimes of violence and crimes against property, including fraud).

VICTIMS

The federal restitution statutes address three questions: Who qualifies as a victim? What crimes trigger restitution authority? What type of injuries or losses does restitution cover? As originally cast, Section 3663 (VWPA) authorized restitution for "any victim" of any crime proscribed in Title 18 of the *United States Code*, but did not define "victim." The Supreme Court read the statute narrowly and held that it authorized restitution only for the crime of conviction; it did not authorize restitution for related charges dropped as part of a plea agreement. Congress responded almost immediately with a more explicit statement of Section 3663's coverage. It replicated and enlarged that statement when it enacted Section 3663A six years later.

Sections 3663 and 3663A authorize restitution orders for the benefit of the victims of the crime of conviction. They augment who may be considered a victim, including persons other than those directly and proximately harmed as a result of the commission of an offense. Sections 3663 and 3663A explain that the term *victim* includes someone harmed by a scheme, conspiracy, or pattern of activity that is an element of the crime of conviction, and twice describe the circumstances under which representatives and others may stand in the shoes of a victim. Finally, sections 3663 and 3663A permit restitution orders for the benefit of anyone identified in a plea agreement.

Absent either a plea bargain or a scheme, conspiracy, or pattern, there must be a close, unbroken connection between a defendant's crime of conviction and the victim's harm. A person is a victim for purposes of sections 3663 and 3663A if he or she has been "directly and proximately harmed" as a consequence of the crime of conviction. A person has not been directly and proximately harmed if his or her injury is only remotely attributable to the crime of conviction or attributable at least in part to an intervening cause unrelated to that offense. The definition of a *victim* for purposes of restitution under sections 3663 and 3663A expands when the crime of conviction has as an element a conspiracy or a scheme or pattern of misconduct. In the case of conspiracy, a defendant may be compelled to make restitution both for the harm caused by his or her own misconduct and for the harm of the foreseeable crimes of his coconspirators. As for the scheme and pattern exception, most federal crimes do not list schemes or patterns among their elements, although the mail fraud, wire fraud, and racketeering statutes do. Thus, in such cases, restitution may include the losses incurred from a different episode of the scheme than the one mentioned in the indictment. Yet the scheme must be the same; victims entitled to restitution do not include those harmed by an otherwise identical scheme but different in time or place than the crime of conviction The courts are divided of what statutes qualify as "scheme, conspiracy or pattern" laws. Some courts say the scheme or pattern must be an element of the crime of conviction; it is not enough that the defendant's crime involves contrivance or repeated related criminality. Others say it is enough; the statute proscribing the crime of conviction need not use the words, "scheme," or "conspiracy," or "pattern."

Although sections 3663 and 3663A employ the same definition of *victim*, they do not authorize restitution for the same crimes. The list of crimes for which Section 3663 permits restitution supplements the list for which Section 3663A demands restitution.

CRIMES — SECTION 3663A (MANDATORY RESTITUTION)

The mandatory restitution of Section 3663A applies upon conviction for (1) a crime of violence, as defined in Section 16; (2) an offense against property under title 18, or under Section 416(a) of the Controlled Substances Act (21 U.S.C. 856(a)), including any offense committed by fraud or deceit; or (3) an offense described in Section 1365 (relating to tampering with consumer products). Three restrictions apply to the mandatory restitution authorized for defendants convicted of the predicate offenses listed in Section 3663A(c)(1)(A). First, there must be an identifiable victim who has suffered physical injury or a pecuniary loss. Second, in the case of the property damage/fraud predicates, restitution need not be ordered when the number of victims makes an order impractical. Third, again in the case of property damage/fraud predicates, restitution need not be ordered when the complexity that restitution would introduce into the sentence process would represent an undue burden. A few other federal statutes authorize restitution. Most apply the procedures that govern sections 3663 and 3663A to a narrower range of crimes but a wider range of losses than sections 3663 and 3663A and their attendant enforcement procedures might otherwise permit.

SECTION 3663 (DISCRETIONARY RESTITUTION)

Section 3663 authorizes restitution when a defendant has been convicted of a crime proscribed under Title 18 of the *United States Code*. It also authorizes restitution when a defendant is convicted of any of several trafficking offenses under the Controlled Substances Act, or of any air safety prohibitions. Finally, restitution may be ordered on the basis of any crime under the laws governing probation and supervisory release generally. Thus, a federal district court may order restitution as a condition of either probation or supervised release, even with respect to crimes for which restitution is not authorized under any of these sections or under sections 3663 or 3663A.

LOSSES

The losses for which restitution may be ordered depend on the statute under which restitution is ordered. Sections 3663 and 3663A make separate provisions for property losses and personal injuries. They call for the return of the property if that provides full victim restitution, and otherwise for compensatory payments. Section 3663 separately authorizes restitution for state agencies in certain trafficking cases if there is no other identifiable victim. Neither section authorizes restitution for a victim's costs associated with the investigation and prosecution of the offense in property loss cases.

PERSONAL INJURIES

Sections 3663 and 3663A have parallel provisions governing the restitution for personal injuries that permit, or in the case of Section 3663A require, compensation for medical expenses, rehabilitation, lost income, prosecution participation costs, and funeral expenses in the event the victim is killed. The medical expenses covered by a restitution order may include those paid on the victim's behalf by a third party, and may include the costs of psychiatric and psychological treatment when the victim has suffered a physical injury. Restitution for lost income extends to both past and future lost income. Both sections authorize restitution for a victim's costs associated with the investigation and prosecution of the offense. Awards for investigative and prosecutorial participation may include relocation expenses for threatened victims, compensation for wages lost while the victim assisted in the investigation, and attorneys' fees related to the child recovery efforts of the victim of an international parental kidnaping. The sections mention child care, attendance at judicial proceedings, and other matters that bespeak a human victim, but the courts have made it clear that other victims are likewise entitled to restitution under the provisions. Governmental entities may be entitled to restitution awards when they are the victims of a qualifying offense, but not for the costs of investigating and prosecuting the offense.

PROCEDURE

Section 3664 supplies the procedure that governs the issuance of restitution orders authorized in Title 18 of the *United States Code* in most instances. The procedure begins upon the conviction of a defendant for a predicate offense, at which point the court directs the probation service to investigate and prepare a report identifying each victim of the offense and the extent of their injuries, damages, or losses. The section calls for prosecutors to provide the probation officer with pertinent information. The officer is also to ask victims to detail the extent and specifics of their predicate crime-related losses. The defendant is obliged to give the officer a complete description of his or her financial situation. The probation officer's report is presented to the court, the defendant, and the prosecutor. The court resolves contested restitution issues by a preponderance of the evidence following a hearing, at which the prosecution bears the burden of establishing the existence and extent of the victims' losses and the defendant bears the burden of questions regarding his or her finances.

Section 3664 is precise when it describes how the court must frame the restitution order. The order must envision full compensation for the losses of each victim without regard to the financial circumstances of the defendant. In its calculation of the amount, manner, and schedule of payment for each victim, however, the court is to consider the defendant's assets, anticipated future income, and other financial obligations. Compensation may be made in lump sum, in-kind payments; installments; or any combination of such methods of payment. In-kind payments may take the form of a return of lost property, replacement in-kind or otherwise, or personal services. When the defendant's financial condition precludes any alternative, the order may call for nominal periodic payments. Several courts have emphasized the importance of the court's close attention to the restitution payment schedule by prohibiting sentencing courts from initially ordering that restitution be paid immediately when it is readily apparent that the defendant is unable to do so, thereby effectively leaving the task of establishing a payment schedule to the probation officer or the Bureau of Prisons.

The court may not take into account the fact that a victim may have been compensated by insurance, forfeiture, civil litigation, or any other alternative form of compensation of his or her injury, loss, or damage. When the government and the probation officer have been unable to determine the full extent of victim losses within 10 days prior to sentencing, they are obligated to inform the court. The court is then to set a date for the final determination of victim losses within 90 days of sentencing. Victims have a limited option to present claims for restitution relating to undiscovered losses thereafter.

There has been more than a slight difference of opinion among the lower federal appellate courts as to how these provisions should be applied, particularly in cases where the time lines have not been observed. Some courts view the time limits as jurisdictional and deny lower courts the authority to order restitution beyond the statutory limits. Some consider them akin to statutes of limitation and permit the time periods to be tolled. Others see the time limits as a device designed for the benefit of victims, not defendants, and for them, the failure to honor the time limits warrants no relief as long as the victim (or the government in the interest of the victim) has no objection and the defendant is given the opportunity to contest. The courts are likewise divided over the question of whether the court may order restitution to be paid to the Crime Victims Fund if the victim refuses to accept it. Should the court determine that more than one defendant contributed to the victim's loss, it may apportion restitution accordingly, or it may make the defendants jointly and severally liable. When defendants are made jointly and severally liable, each is liable for the entire amount, but the victim is entitled to no more than what is required to be made whole, regardless of what portion each of the defendants ultimately contributes. Section 3664(i) declares that when it comes to restitution, the United States is to be served last. The provision is cited most often to confirm that under the appropriate circumstances, the government and its departments and agencies may be considered victims for restitution purposes. Where the government is not a victim, however, the forfeiture laws may operate to deplete any assets from which restitution might otherwise have been paid. On the other hand, the defendant is not entitled to have the restitution award offset by the value of the forfeited property, unless the victim is the governmental entity for whose benefit the property is confiscated.

Section 3664(j) permits a court to order restitution to third parties who, as insurers or otherwise, have assumed some or all of the victim's losses, although in such cases, the victim must be fully compensated first. Section 3664(j) also supplies the only explicit offset for the defendant's restitution obligations. A restitution award may be reduced after issuance by any amounts that the victim later receives in the course of related federal or state civil litigation. Nevertheless, the victim, the defendant, or the government may seek to have a restitution order amended to reflect the defendant's changed economic circumstances. The changed economic circumstances envisioned in Section 3664(k) do not include anticipated future changes nor a later, better-informed understanding of the defendant's financial condition at the time of sentence.

There are several means to enforce a restitution order. When restitution is a condition of probation or supervised release, failure to make restitution may provide the grounds for revocation. Moreover, a restitution order operates as a lien on the defendant's property that remains in effect for 20 years. The government may also use garnishment and the other collection mechanisms of the Federal Debt Collection Procedures Act to enforce a restitution order. A victim may also use a restitution order to secure a lien against the defendant's property to ensure the payment of restitution. In addition, the victims' rights provisions of 18 U.S.C. 3771 entitle a victim to "full and timely restitution as provided in law," a right the section makes enforceable through a liberalized form of mandamus. In most instances, the victim may also sue the defendant based on the conduct that led to his conviction and the issuance of the restitution order. During the course of such civil litigation, the defendant may be precluded from denying the facts that formed the basis of his conviction.

Abatement

In a criminal law context, the lower federal courts have generally taken the view that the death of a defendant at any time prior to the determination of his or her final direct appeal abates all underlying proceedings; appeals are dismissed as moot, convictions are overturned, indictments are dismissed, and abated convictions cannot be used in related civil litigation against the estate — all as if the defendant was never criminally charged. It might seem from this that a restitution order would abate as well, but there is no consensus among the lower federal courts on the issue.

INDEX

A

B

C

M

N

O

P

R

S

T

U

V

W